Drama Activi for the Early Years

Promoting Learning across the Foundation Stage Curriculum

Debbie Chalmers

Brilliant
PUBLICATIONS

We hope you enjoy using this book. If you would like further information on other books or e-resources published by Brilliant Publications, please write to the address given below or look on our website: www.brilliantpublications.co.uk.

Foundation Blocks series
Communication and Language with Literacy
Physical Development with Expressive Arts and Design
Personal, Social and Emotional Development with Understanding the World and Mathematics

Activities for 3–5 Year Olds series
All About Us
Caring and Sharing
Colours
Families
Food
Gardening
Pets
Shopping
Water
Weather

Other titles
Phonic Limericks
Play Activities for the Early Years
Science and Technology for the Early Years
Creative Activities for the Early Years
Games for the Early Years
Preschool Art: It's the process not the product!

Published by Brilliant Publications
Unit 10
Sparrow Hall Farm
Edlesborough
Dunstable
Bedfordshire
LU6 2ES, UK

E mail: info@brilliantpublications.co.uk
Website: www.brilliantpublications.co.uk
Tel: 01525 222292

The name Brilliant Publications and the logo are registered trademarks.

Written by Debbie Chalmers
Illustrated by Cathy Hughes

Contents

Activities

Activity	Page no	Early Learning Goals Addressed						
		CL	PSED	PD	L	M	UW	EAD
Movement/Dance								
Pass it on	21	✔	✔	✔				✔
Monkeys in the trees	22	✔	✔				✔	✔
Octopus's garden	23		✔	✔				✔
Little bird	24	✔	✔	✔			✔	✔
Move and freeze	25	✔	✔	✔				✔
Stand up, sit down	26	✔	✔	✔				✔
Munching mini-beasts	27	✔		✔			✔	✔
One brick at a time	28	✔	✔	✔				✔
Contrasts	29	✔	✔	✔				✔
A turn to dance	30		✔					✔
Over the river	31		✔	✔				✔
Up the hill	32	✔	✔	✔	✔			✔
Puddle jumping	33		✔	✔		✔		✔
Musical hats	34	✔	✔				✔	✔
Cross the bridge	35	✔			✔			✔
Acting/Mime								
Guess who I am	36	✔	✔					✔
Make a machine	37	✔	✔	✔			✔	✔
Make a face	38		✔	✔				✔
Raiding the nest	39		✔					✔
Dig a hole	40		✔					✔
Welcome to my home	41	✔	✔	✔	✔		✔	✔
The wind blows	42	✔		✔				✔

Activity	Page no	Early Learning Goals Addressed						
		CL	PSED	PD	L	M	UW	EAD
Weather forecast	43	✔	✔					✔
Creating a storm	44		✔				✔	✔
Capture the scene	45						✔	✔
Open the box	46	✔	✔	✔				✔
Join in for effect	47		✔	✔				✔
Singing								
Body language	48	✔	✔					✔
Atishoo, atishoo	49	✔	✔	✔				✔
Counting down	50	✔	✔			✔		✔
Make a noise	51		✔	✔				✔
Play that tune	52	✔	✔					✔
Walk or run	53	✔	✔	✔				✔
Nimble fingers	54		✔	✔		✔		✔
Rhyme time	55	✔	✔					✔
Speech								
Pleased to meet you	56	✔	✔	✔			✔	
Do you hear what I say?	57	✔	✔	✔	✔		✔	
Food on the move	58		✔					✔
Let's build a house	59	✔	✔	✔				
What's happening in the garden?	60	✔	✔	✔				✔
Answer me	61	✔	✔		✔			
Speak in character	62	✔	✔		✔			✔
Story posters	63	✔	✔	✔	✔		✔	✔
Square rhymes	64	✔	✔	✔	✔			
Listening								
Make an echo	65		✔	✔		✔		✔
Balancing act	66	✔	✔	✔		✔		✔
Sailing into the wind	67	✔	✔	✔		✔		✔
Loud or soft?	68	✔	✔	✔		✔		✔
Movement match	69	✔	✔	✔		✔		✔
Chinese dragons	70	✔	✔				✔	✔
What was that word?	71	✔	✔	✔	✔			
Cue for a rhyme	72	✔	✔	✔	✔		✔	
Building a rhyme	73	✔	✔	✔	✔		✔	
Confidence								
Follow that horse	74	✔	✔					✔
Life cycles	75	✔	✔	✔			✔	✔
Order and direction	76	✔	✔	✔			✔	✔
Jump up	77	✔	✔	✔			✔	✔
Thank you for watching	78	✔	✔	✔				✔

Activity	Page no	Early Learning Goals Addressed						
		CL	PSED	PD	L	M	UW	EAD
What shall we wear?	79		✔	✔			✔	✔
Building site	80	✔	✔	✔			✔	✔
Tree directions	81	✔	✔	✔		✔	✔	✔
Group work								
Hungry snake	82			✔			✔	✔
Follow the trail	83		✔	✔			✔	✔
Corners	84	✔	✔	✔				✔
Animal patterns	85	✔	✔			✔		✔
Roll the dice	86	✔	✔	✔		✔		✔
Beehives	87	✔	✔	✔		✔		✔
Magic rings	88		✔	✔		✔		✔
Where should I be?	89	✔	✔	✔		✔	✔	✔
Rainbow dance	90	✔	✔	✔				✔
Craftwork								
Portraits	91		✔	✔		✔	✔	✔
A meal out	92	✔	✔	✔	✔	✔		✔
Special times	93	✔					✔	✔
Hide and seek	94	✔	✔				✔	✔
Make a scene	95		✔	✔				✔
Bring on the rain	96	✔	✔					✔
Firework night	97				✔	✔		✔
There's a troll	98	✔		✔			✔	✔
Mask the effect	99	✔	✔	✔		✔		✔
Puppet theatre	100	✔	✔	✔				✔

Introduction

Young children are naturally dramatic. Their world is full of new and interesting experiences and they find excitement in the smallest of things. They love to pretend to be characters or animals, to explore and act out stories, to talk, sing and move within a group and to copy each other. Responsive practitioners can encourage this type of play by offering opportunities for drama activities, adapted to suit individual children or groups. Specific activities can be planned and offered at group times and others may be suggested whenever a child or a small group is ready to develop their role-play, language or movement.

Inclusion and confidence for all children

Drama is very inclusive and can be accessed individually by a group of children who may be working at a range of different levels. Experienced practitioners can use it to calm and direct those who are excitable and to encourage those who are less confident, while getting to know each child and identifying any who may need extra support. Drama is a social and cooperative activity which promotes teamwork and sensitivity to others and also encourages children to gradually take a greater responsibility for their own needs and to develop the ability to speak confidently and politely.

Young children with a variety of special needs, particularly those with Autism, Asperger Syndrome and other communication difficulties, benefit from participating in dramatic activities from a very young age. Through drama, they can develop vital self-confidence within their peer groups, improve their social skills and practise understanding and expressing feelings and emotions, enabling them to learn to play, pretend, share, cooperate and interact with other children during their pre-school years. Having these skills in place allows them to make a smoother transition into primary education, with a reduced need for specialist support and a greater ability to enjoy and take advantage of the new opportunities offered to them.

Developing skills and attitudes

It is valuable for all children to pretend, act out and discuss feelings and emotions, to create a range of movements and positions with their bodies and to hold hands with other children, to cooperate and participate in group work, to be willing to try new activities and to understand when and how to stop. Mime and expression, movement and dance, listening skills, speech and language, rhythm and singing and performing to others can all bring great pleasure and a sense of achievement to children, while supporting their progress and creating balanced and confident individuals. Practising established skills, alongside learning new ones, will prepare children for later life, developing focusing and concentration abilities and appropriate attitudes within a group.

Creativity through art and music

Expressive and performing arts encourage creativity in every dimension. Children's dramatic learning should always be reinforced, enhanced and developed by opportunities for craftwork and music, allowing visual, aural and kinaesthetic learners to benefit and progress equally. With support, children can create their own costumes, props, set pieces and backcloths to set the scene for any drama workshop or performance work. They can choose instruments and other sounds to use while acting, appropriate music or songs to include and sound effects to symbolize particular actions or events, weather, characters or animals.

Children are interested in all types of music and their listening shouldn't be restricted to 'children's songs'. Use everything from popular and classical tunes to rock and roll, jazz and brass bands, and especially introduce them to songs and tunes from all the great musical stage shows from as early an age as possible. Practitioners should share some of the music that they like, as, when the adults are enjoying a song, the children will also enjoy it more. (However, do check all of the lyrics for suitability before letting the children hear a song.) Children can often be heard singing or humming parts of the songs that their families listen to at home.

Positive experiences can be extended when children are encouraged to make pictures, models, books and displays about completed drama projects and to talk about them, or to make props to take home so that they can lead and recreate the activities with their own families. Parents may be encouraged to bring in resources to develop, extend or add to a project. Children love poring over the pictures in adult non-fiction books about animals, vehicles, machines, plants and other suitable topics and often enjoy encyclopedias just as much as the simple non-fiction books that are written specifically for them. They don't need to be able to read or understand the text to absorb information in this visual way.

Equipment and resources

Most drama activities need only enough space to run successfully and require minimal equipment and resources that will usually be already available within an early years setting. An important part of the practitioner's role is to provide a wealth of resources that children may use to develop all of their ideas. These will include an exciting range of items, offering assorted colours, textures, shapes, sizes and forms. Some will be craft pieces purchased cheaply from education suppliers, such as feathers, sequins, stickers and paper fasteners, but many will be found and recycled items, donated by staff and parents, such as cereal boxes, string, wool and fabric scraps. Particularly useful items to collect and maintain a supply of are cardboard tubes from kitchen rolls, paper plates and shirring or cord elastic. Basic art and craft equipment must always be available in quantities sufficient for all the children, so that they may use paper, card, pens, scissors, glue and paint whenever they need them.

Children should have access to music equipment that is safe and simple to operate, so that they may choose to listen to music or songs or to record and play back their own voices or other sounds during free play sessions. They may then choose to use these in independent role play or to share them with the larger group during drama activities. If possible, also provide torches or lamps and hand held microphones for older or more experienced children, to allow them to enhance their developing creative and technical skills within free play and performances for their families. Provide accessible, safe storage for costumes, props and backcloths that children make for themselves, so that they may re-use or adapt them whenever they choose to. Make sure they know that they can move chairs or ask for help with other furniture if they need scenery or set in a particular place.

Themes and activities

The activities in this book are intended to form a practical resource for practitioners to use whenever they have an opportunity to engage in drama with the children in their care. Learning opportunities and links to the Early Learning Goals of the revised EYFS are clearly listed, to assist in the assessing and recording of children's progress and development. All activities can be easily adapted to suit smaller or larger groups and practitioners may choose confidently for their children, according to theme or learning objectives, whether they wish to work with 3–4 children or a group of 20–30 children. A small group may work with one or two adults. In larger groups, aim for a ratio of one adult per 4–6 children for 2–3 year olds or one adult per 6–10 children for 4–5 year olds. The length of time devoted to any activity can also be adapted to fit the time available. Activities can be led by one or two practitioners, while others either join in to support particular children or stand back to observe and assess.

A variety of stories, songs, rhymes and music are mentioned throughout the book. These are listed, with page numbers, on pages 104–105. These popular storybooks may already be available within the setting, or other favourites could be used instead. Some of the songs (and instrumental tracks for some well-known and traditional songs) are available to download from the Brilliant Publications' website as e-resources for a small fee. However, practitioners may have their own repertoires and favourites and could substitute them with any appropriate songs, tunes and CDs of their choice.

There are many ways of building confidence and imagination in children and this is a gradual but rewarding process that practitioners must be aware of throughout the early years. It is important for children to learn how to express themselves clearly, to practise speech and movement skills, to participate in role-play situations and to develop imagination and flexibility, in order to build self-confidence and good self-esteem. Although they will seek to do this for themselves when they play, opportunities to participate in both adult-led and child-initiated drama will give them a head start and the benefits will stay with them throughout their lives.

How Drama Activities can Contribute to the Prime and Specific Areas

Communication and Language

Children develop and improve their communication and language skills through an understanding of speech, but also of posture, body language, mime, taking cues, responding to others and self confidence. A variety of drama activities can offer these opportunities. These include:

*   Listening and concentrating, within a group, while stories and rhymes are read or told by an adult, then participating in discussion and offering relevant comments

*   Taking cues, while working with well-known rhymes or stories, to supply words to fill in gaps left by the adult or to correct deliberate mistakes, or to carry out an agreed action or movement every time a particular word is heard

*   Being silent and still for short periods, in response to spoken or musical cues

*   Participating in mime sequences and discussions, to impart a message and express themselves clearly, both non-verbally and verbally

*   Answering questions about their own imaginative sequences, to explain how and why things happened or what characters were thinking

*   Introducing themselves to each other and to adults, using polite and confident speech and body language

*   Taking and following instructions, offering enhancing ideas and working cooperatively within large or small groups

*   Responding to directions in order to participate in a group game, such as moving to a particular corner, performing an action or taking a turn

*   Enunciating clearly while speaking rhymes or taking part in delivering speeches or dialogues in character

*   Re-telling stories within a group, or narrating them while acting them out

*   Making decisions and wishes known by expressing them clearly in polite language and listening and responding to the ideas and wishes of others

*   Using mime and body language as a new form of communication and understanding where it is particularly appropriate, such as making a bow or a curtsey at the end of an activity.

Personal, Social and Emotional Development

Responding to others, interaction and teamwork are vital to successful drama. Children may learn to work together and display sensitivity to each other's needs if offered opportunities to refine and practise these skills through taking part in appropriate activities. These include:

*   Displaying self-confidence in trying new activities, talking about what they liked or didn't like and asking for help if needed

*   Portraying their expressions and feelings and guessing those of others, using mime and discussion

* Participating in ring and group games, in which each person will choose or be chosen in turn, supported by adults who will maintain fairness

* Working within both larger and smaller groups to create sequences, scenes, songs and movements, sometimes leading and sometimes following

* Talking about and receiving support and encouragement in controlling physical and personality traits, such as nervousness, shyness, bossiness, quick temper or frustration, in order to participate constructively

* Remembering rules and following adult role models in order to understand the need to wait, share and take turns and to display patience and calmness while working on a group activity

* Choosing their own directions, regardless of 'friendship groups', developing the confidence to work with anyone in the group and to only copy others when appropriate

* Adjusting behaviour to suit different situations, such as individual work, small group work and working within a large group or class

* Speaking out or performing non-verbally before a familiar group

* Organizing activities in cooperation with others, being sensitive to the needs of each member of the group and including everyone's ideas

* Working together to form and maintain positive relationships with adults and peers, despite occasional mild disagreements

* Understanding the uses of symbolism in role-play and acting and when certain stereotypes in costume or speech may be acceptable in order to make a character obvious to an audience, such as a burglar wearing a striped outfit or an old person using a walking stick.

Physical Development

Children need to develop confident control and coordination of their bodies before they can succeed in challenges in more specific areas. Drama activities provide many opportunities for children to explore and develop their physical skills. These include:

* Basic whole body movements, such as walking, running, hopping, jumping, stepping, striding, marching, tiptoeing, crawling, slithering, rolling and 'falling'

* Moving in different directions, including forwards, sideways and backwards

* Developing spatial awareness and being able to find their own spaces or move around in a space, allowing room for others around them, confidently negotiating a safe pathway and avoiding collisions or confusions

* Creating dance movements in response to music, such as shaking, wriggling, swaying, spinning, twirling, jumping, marching, stepping or gymnastics

* Creating rhythms with the body in response to music, songs or rhymes, such as clapping, tapping, stamping, nodding, clicking fingers and standing up and sitting down

* Finger rhymes and action songs, which may be performed with the hands or the whole body, sitting in a group or circle or standing in spaces

* Dressing and undressing, independently or with support, in costumes and accessories

* Attending to personal needs, such as hunger, thirst, hygiene and using the toilet, when convenient, without allowing them to take over or distract from their dramatic play.

Literacy

There can be many opportunities for developing and using emerging reading and writing skills in drama, even amongst the youngest children. These include:

* Reading their own names and those of their friends within lists, in order to find their places within groups and activities

* Finding their own name cards, in order to place them appropriately to choose their own activities

* Selecting appropriate books and other resources for a theme by reading titles and simple information

* Sharing books, pictures and posters to discuss, tell or read stories and rhymes, then acting them out together

* Reading song lyrics, scripts, lines, speeches, dialogues or directions at whichever level each child has reached, with support and encouragement from adults as appropriate to individuals

* Reading instructions and guidelines for group activities and related artwork and craft projects

* Drawing and writing about a theme or project, or what they like about drama, and making their contributions into displays

* Making posters and notices, handbills and flyers to advertise their performances, both within everyday group work and when displaying drama work to parents and carers

* Dancing or moving to music and sitting down or freezing whenever the music stops

* Balancing on different parts of the body, such as on hands and feet or on one leg

* Creating postures and movements to suit particular characters or actions, such as old people or animals, digging or swimming

* Handling props when acting in character, such as hats, bags, wands or swords

* Using props in music, movement and dance activities, such as percussion instruments, hoops or ribbons

* Using commercial apparatus or their own efforts with furniture, outdoor equipment or recycled materials to create climbing and balancing scenes within stories, such as bridges, walls or castle battlements

* Participating in art and craftwork activities to create items of costume and props

* Drawing and writing signs and notices to enhance role-play and performances

* Creating alternative endings for stories, or adding scenes that might have happened before or after the written story

* Making books of favourite stories, rhymes or songs, consisting of pages written and illustrated by different children and collected and bound by an adult

* Taking their own notes while working in groups and using them as an aid to remembering their ideas over several sessions or to read out as explanations when performing their work to others

* Writing song lyrics, scripts, lines, speeches, dialogues or directions at whichever level each child has reached, with support and encouragement from adults as appropriate to individuals.

Mathematics

Children can learn and consolidate mathematical skills, learning about numbers, shapes, space and measures in a practical and enjoyable way, through a variety of drama activities. These include:

* Number rhymes and songs, involving counting both up and down in ones or twos and recognizing threes, fives and tens, using fingers or whole body movements

* Making themselves into small groups of three, four or five etc, as suggested by adults, in order to carry out certain short activities

* Counting and remembering the numbers of steps or other moves in dance or movement routines and sequences

* Considering how much space they need to safely make particular movements and allowing enough room for others around them

* Exploring positional language by following directions and instructions involving different concepts, such as in front of or behind, under or over, up or down, around or between

* Comparing distances and speeds through playing games involving opposites, such as giant strides and tiptoe steps or running quickly and creeping slowly

* Creating a speech, song, scene or movement within a time limit, either individually or as a small group, and then performing to each other in turn.

Understanding the World

Drama, music and dance span all cultures and bring people of the world together. Children can gain an understanding of different people, communities and beliefs through exploring celebrations, festivals and traditions. They can also understand concepts of the natural world and changes within their environment and recognize some uses of technology through dramatic activities. These include:

* Finding out about and exploring music and dances from a variety of cultures, using books, pictures, posters, DVDs and the Internet

* Imitating some of the musical rhythms with percussion instruments

* Having a go at copying some of the dances and movements, especially if it is possible to invite

any people with the appropriate skills to visit the setting to demonstrate (parents, carers, other family members or friends, amateur or professional groups)

* Dressing up in traditional outfits and acting in character (avoiding stereotyping)

* Learning useful words in other languages, such as greetings, and using them in speech activities with peers and adults

* Miming and acting as different people, considering ages, occupations and relationships

* Using mime, expression and acting skills to display contrasts, similarities and differences, between people, animals, plants and other living things

* Exploring life cycles of plants and creatures through discussing and acting out the changes and different stages

* Pretending to be machines, either individually or in small groups, imagining and creating appropriate positions, postures and movements

* Using CD players and tape recorders as devices for playing stories or music and for recording and playing back their own sounds and voices

* Learning to use microphones to amplify voices and sounds, speaking at a correct volume, holding them at the right distance and in an appropriate position and operating them safely

* Understanding the uses and benefits of lighting, curtains, backdrops and scenery for creating desired effects when performing, and how to use a stage where one is available.

Expressive Arts and Design

Drama is an integral part of expressive arts and involves a great deal of design. Children can explore a variety of media and materials and develop their imaginations to the full if offered enough opportunities to engage in

drama and performing arts with the support and encouragement of interested, enthusiastic and experienced adults. One or more practitioners within a setting may have the appropriate experience and confidence to lead in this area, to the benefit of the other staff and all of the children. If this is not the case, they should consider inviting in other adults who are able to demonstrate and lead the types of activities that practitioners may then learn to use and build upon for themselves in their drama work with the children. These include:

* Learning and singing new and familiar songs and making up their own

* Learning different steps and movements and creating their own dances

* Using percussion instruments to accompany singing, dance or movement

* Creating sound effects to enhance songs, rhymes, stories or scenes, using voices, bodies, objects, materials and instruments

* Exploring the uses of props, such as ribbons, sticks, balls, hoops, scarves or swathes of fabric, in creating effects and impressions

* Using craft materials to make their own props, either smaller items such as cups, lanterns, play money or tools, or larger pieces of set such as

boats, cars or windows, to use when acting out a story or rhyme

* Creating their own masks, hats, headdresses, helmets, wigs, cloaks and other costume items, using craft materials and fabric pieces

* Finding or making and using pieces of costume, equipment and props specific to a particular character or story, especially in superhero or historical role-play, such as swords, shields, wristbands, belts, pet animals, snakes, horses, vehicles and machines

* Designing and drawing large 'backdrops' for performances as a group, using old sheets and fabric markers or rolls of frieze paper and paints or pens

* Making puppets and using them to re-tell stories or encourage more confident speech

* Creating and developing characters, actions and scenarios in role-play

* Exploring and practising different sounds, voices, phrases and speeches appropriate to a variety of characters and animals

* Re-telling and re-enacting favourite stories

* Absorbing new situations and challenges from adults and acting out 'what happened next'.

Areas of Development and Skills for Drama in the Early Years

Drama is usually taught through the following main areas of development and skills, each delivering a number of learning objectives, which overlap smoothly with each other:

* Movement/Dance
* Acting/Mime
* Singing
* Speech
* Listening
* Confidence
* Group work

Whether in frequent sessions or regular classes for very young children or in single workshops for older ones, they are usually taught in this order of ascending difficulty, starting with Movement/Dance, to allow children to progress and achieve as they mature and develop or as they gain in skills and confidence.

Craft work is also considered a vital part of creative and expressive development and provides important links and extensions to many drama activities.

The activities in this book are grouped into these eight areas, although skills from other areas can be learned for each one and these are also listed.

Practitioners and teachers planning and providing drama activities and experiences for children in the Early Years Foundation Stage should be aware of appropriate learning objectives for this age group in each of the main areas. They are listed in the chart on pages 15–20, along with their links to the Early Learning Goals of the Department for Education's Statutory Framework for the Early Years Foundation Stage (September 2012).

Key to Early Learning Goals

The following codes are used on the contents pages, in the chart on pages 15–20 and in the learning objectives listed on each activity page.

CL	Communication and Literacy
CL–LA	Listening and Attention
CL–U	Understanding
CL–S	Speaking
PSED	Personal, Social and Emotional Development
PSED–MR	Making Relationships
PSED–SCSA	Self-confidence and Self-awareness
PSED–MFB	Managing Feelings and Behaviour
PD	Physical Development
PD–MH	Moving and Handling
PD-HSC	Health and Self-care
L	Literacy
L–R	Reading
L–W	Writing
M	Mathematics
M–N	Numbers
M–SSM	Shape, Space and Measures
UW	Understanding the World
UW–PC	People and Communities
UW–W	The World
UW–T	Technology
EAD	Expressive Arts and Design
EAD–EUMM	Exploring and Using Materials and Media
EAD–BI	Being Imaginative

Links to the Early Learning Goals

	CL			PSED			PD		L		M		UW			EAD	
	LA	U	S	MR	SCSA	MFB	MH	HSC	R	W	N	SSM	PC	W	T	EUMM	BI
Movement/Dance																	
Listen carefully and imitate and create movement in response to types of music																✓	✓
Move rhythmically and show awareness of tempo and mood																✓	
Communicate meaning and express feelings through movement, mime and dance in various styles																	✓
Explore and learn how sounds can be changed																✓	
Maintain attention, concentrate and move or stop quietly when appropriate	✓																
Initiate new combinations of movement and gesture to express and respond to feelings and ideas																	✓
Interact as a member of a group to develop and act out a narrative or storyline through dance																	✓
Portray different characters through a variety of movements and actions																	✓
Memorize simple dances and confidently perform them to others, individually or within a group					✓											✓	
Move freely and with pleasure and confidence in a range of ways							✓										
Negotiate space successfully within a group, adjusting speed or changing direction to avoid obstacles or collisions							✓										
Match movements and actions to the space available							✓										
Develop good control and coordination in large and small movements							✓										
Learn and use vocabulary of movement and controlled effort							✓										
Manage own personal needs successfully and offer to help others								✓									
Acting/Mime																	
Re-enact real, first-hand experiences through imaginative role-play																	✓
Work cooperatively with others to act out a familiar part of a storyline																	✓
Develop and act out an experience, a storyline or a narrative, working cooperatively within a group, and practise skills to perform before others with confidence					✓												✓

	CL			PSED			PD		L		M		UW			EAD	
	LA	U	S	MR	SCSA	MFB	MH	HSC	R	W	N	SSM	PC	W	T	EUMM	BI
Acting/Mime (cont)																	
Explore and develop skills of characterization within a small group, using different forms of language and intonation to imagine and recreate roles and experiences			✓														
Portray characters and emotions through mime and expressive movement, understanding that the body can be used for communication																	✓
Create simple representations of events, people, creatures or objects to develop a watchable movement sequence within the boundaries of a given storyline or narrative																	✓
Thank the audience after a performance through body language, without need for speech																	✓
Share ideas within a group and develop imagination around a theme, showing sensitivity to others' needs and feelings and forming positive relationships				✓													
Confidently try a new activity and explore an unfamiliar theme					✓												
Maintain concentration and participation in a large group activity and cooperate in a game that requires turn taking and understanding of rules				✓	✓												
Operate simple technological equipment for use in musical and/or dramatic activities															✓		
Singing																	
Memorize simple songs, including words, tunes and appropriate actions, and sing them in unison with others, maintaining a steady speed and volume																✓	
Memorize simple songs, including words, tunes and appropriate actions, and sing them individually, performing before others with confidence					✓											✓	
Add to a growing repertoire of familiar songs and dances to be used in a variety of situations and activities																✓	
Sing familiar songs with confidence and experiment with ways of changing them, by selecting appropriate accompanying sounds and playing instruments to enhance performance																✓	
Explore and develop skills of characterization within a small group, by representing own ideas, thoughts and feelings through music, dance and role-play while acting out a familiar storyline within a song																	✓

	CL			PSED			PD		L		M		UW			EAD	
	LA	U	S	MR	SCSA	MFB	MH	HSC	R	W	N	SSM	PC	W	T	EUMM	BI
Singing (cont)																	
Make up simple songs and rhythms and adapt familiar ones to fit particular themes																	✓
Accurately anticipate and join in with repeated refrains and key phrases in songs, or respond with relevant actions	✓																
Take cues to imitate, fill in or continue words or phrases in a song	✓																
Use intonation and different voices in action and character songs			✓														
Confidently use songs and rhymes that involve number names, counting on and counting back in ones, twos, fives and tens, using fingers or whole body actions											✓						
Speech																	
Use language to imagine and recreate ideas and experiences for acting and role-play			✓														
Talk about and explain the symbolic use of furniture and objects in pretend situations and as props			✓														
Use talk to organize, sequence and clarify thinking, ideas, feelings and events when planning scenarios or performances			✓														
Explain own knowledge and understanding, ask appropriate questions of others, take account of others' ideas and resolve conflicts through compromise				✓													
Experiment with words and sounds, rhythm, intonation, character voices and speeches, sound effects and differences in speed and volume in songs, rhymes and stories			✓						✓								
Speak confidently within a familiar group and take turns to initiate discussion, describe an activity or perform a speech, song or rhyme, asking for help if needed					✓												
Improve enunciation, in order to express words, ideas and messages clearly, showing awareness of listeners' needs			✓														
Join in with repeated refrains and anticipate key events and phrases in rhymes and stories	✓																
Take cues confidently to fill in the missing word or phrase in a known rhyme, story or song, or to speak in character to continue a storyline or narrative									✓								
Speak clearly in unison			✓		✓												
Speak clearly individually			✓		✓												
Improve voice projection			✓		✓												

	CL			PSED			PD		L		M		UW			EAD	
	LA	U	S	MR	SCSA	MFB	MH	HSC	R	W	N	SSM	PC	W	T	EUMM	BI
Listening																	
Listen to stories, songs or rhymes with increasing attention and recall, in order to discuss and recreate all or parts of them	✓																
Listen to songs and sing back what is heard, line by line, in order to learn them by heart, for immediate use or to add to a repertoire																✓	
Copy and tap out simple repeated rhythms and identify them as familiar names, words, phrases, rhymes or songs																✓	
Count beats and reproduce specific numbers of beats as necessary											✓						
Notice changes in what is heard	✓																
Observe silences as part of a group, following agreed ideas and rules					✓												
Explore the different sounds of instruments and use them appropriately to enhance performances																✓	
Recognize rhythm, rhyme and alliteration and use them in activities									✓								
Initiate discussion and conversation and attend to and take account of what others say, in order to plan and create a scenario or performance				✓													
Operate simple technological equipment to allow repeated listening to songs, music, sounds or stories															✓		
Confidence																	
Think independently and offer ideas and opinions confidently to a group			✓		✓												
Understand a new concept and verbalize thinking and understanding		✓	✓														
Have an awareness of and an interest in cultural and language differences or jobs and occupations													✓				
Gain an awareness of the cultures and beliefs of others													✓				
Work, speak and listen appropriately as a member of a group, showing sensitivity to others' needs and feelings and responding with consideration				✓													
Lead a group confidently				✓	✓												
Improve confidence and social skills through participation in a large group activity				✓		✓	✓										
Develop and use skills and explore concepts and ideas, embracing challenge and greater stimulation																	✓

	CL			PSED			PD		L		M		UW			EAD	
	LA	U	S	MR	SCSA	MFB	MH	HSC	R	W	N	SSM	PC	W	T	EUMM	BI
Group work																	
Participate in a large group game or activity, understanding the need for rules and cooperation to ensure everybody's enjoyment				✓		✓											
Remember rules and aims of the game or activity and try various different strategies				✓		✓											
Follow instructions involving several ideas or actions		✓															
Follow simple safety rules, tackle new challenges and manage appropriate risks					✓		✓	✓									
Know that physical exercise can contribute to good health								✓									
Count aloud reliably using numbers 1–10 or 1–20 in order while playing a group game, to make a number of steps or jumps or to wait for a number of seconds											✓						
Describe sizes, positions, distances or times through participating in group or ring games												✓					
Follow treasure hunts or trails in character, exploring an outdoor or indoor area as an animal or a person from a story														✓		✓	
Use positional language, count steps and talk about distances and directions														✓			
Select and use technology for particular purposes															✓		
Craftwork																	
Construct with a purpose in mind, using a variety of resources																✓	
Use simple tools and techniques competently and appropriately																✓	
Explore and experiment to create different colours or textures																✓	
Understand that different media can be combined to create new effects																✓	
Safely use and explore a variety of materials, tools and techniques, experimenting with colour, design, texture, form and function																✓	
Use skills to explore concepts and ideas through representations																✓	
Use available resources to create costume pieces and props to support role-play																	✓
Capture experiences and responses with a range of media																	✓
Choose particular colours or materials to use for a purpose																	✓

	CL			PSED			PD		L		M		UW			EAD	
	LA	U	S	MR	SCSA	MFB	MH	HSC	R	W	N	SSM	PC	W	T	EUMM	BI
Craft work (cont)																	
Create simple representations of events, people and objects																	✓
Use media and materials in original ways to suit different uses or purposes																	✓
Represent own ideas, thoughts and feelings through art and design																	✓
Use a simple program on a computer to produce text, pictures and designs															✓		
Celebrate diversity, avoiding stereotypes and challenging any negative attitudes													✓				
Use and name shapes appropriately in creative tasks												✓					
Use identifiable letters and phonic knowledge to communicate meaning										✓							
Write own name and labels and captions										✓							
Handle equipment and tools effectively, including pencils for drawing and writing							✓										
Confidently try new activities, choose resources independently and say when do or don't need help					✓												
Work cooperatively, taking turns to use equipment and sharing resources				✓													
Manage own basic personal and hygiene needs successfully								✓									

Pass it on

Themes

* Creatures/Animals/Birds/Plants
* Food/Drinks/Meals

Skills

* Movement/Dance
* Acting/Mime
* Listening
* Confidence
* Group work

Equipment/Resources

A safe, clear space in which adults and children can sit comfortably in a circle, an item that makes a noise, such as a maraca or a bunch of keys

Activity

Gather the group of practitioners and children and invite them to sit in a circle. Tell them that you have a small, soft hamster in your hands and you would like everybody to meet it, but it is quite shy and frightened of loud noises and quick movements.

Stroke the pretend hamster gently and then very carefully pass it to the child on your right. Ask him to stroke the hamster and pass it carefully to the person on his right.

Encourage all of the group members to take the hamster in turn and pass it on, until the child on your left gives it back to you. Praise the children for being kind and careful.

Extensions/Variations

Repeat the game, pretending that you are passing around a hot food item, such as a jacket potato, or a cold drink full of ice cubes. You now need to pass very quickly, but ensure that all children do take the pretend object and pass it to their neighbour, rather than grabbing for it, throwing it or dropping it.

Play at passing around a real item that makes a noise, such as a maraca or a bunch of keys, and try not to make a sound as you move and take the object. If a child makes a sound accidently, just smile and say 'shush', but, if it happens on purpose, ask him to try again and to be even more careful this time.

Learning objectives/Early Learning Goals

* Maintain attention, concentrate and move or stop quietly when appropriate (CL–LA)
* Develop good control and coordination in large and small movements (PD–MH)
* Confidently try a new activity and explore an unfamiliar theme (PSED–SCSA)
* Observe silences as part of a group, following agreed ideas and rules (PSED–MFB)
* Develop and use skills and explore concepts and ideas, embracing challenge and greater stimulation (EAD–BI)
* Participate in a large group activity, understanding the need for rules and cooperation to ensure everybody's enjoyment (PSED–MR, MFB)

Monkeys in the trees

Themes
* Creatures/Animals/Birds/Plants
* Food/Drinks/Meals

Skills
* Movement/Dance
* Listening
* Group work
* Craftwork

Equipment/Resources
A clear space with a safe, clean floor surface, in which children can move around easily; a large quantity of plastic or wooden 'play fruits' of different types; tape recorder and blank tape; cardboard tubes; wool, twine or raffia; green crêpe or tissue paper; coloured card and paper; scissors and sticky tape

Activity
Scatter the fruits all over the floor. Ask practitioners to stand in spaces with their arms raised, as trees.

Invite children to be monkeys and to jump and 'swing' around, collecting fruits and pretending to eat them.

At frequent intervals, a practitioner or a recorded sound should roar like a tiger. Encourage children to drop the fruits and run to hide behind a 'tree' whenever they hear the tiger, then to creep out for more food when they think it's safe again.

Extensions/Variations
Vary this game to suit any theme. It could be set in a rainforest, a zoo or a wood and children could be parrots, snakes, mice or hedgehogs hiding from crocodiles, owls or foxes.

Incorporate the game into the re-enactment of a popular story, such as when the wolf comes in Little Red Riding Hood or The Three Little Pigs.

Provide a tape recorder and support children in recording and playing back roars and other sounds created with their own voices.

Make jungle or forest trees from cardboard tubes, attaching strips of green crêpe or tissue paper, coloured card and paper and wool, twine or raffia with sticky tape.

Learning objectives/Early Learning Goals
* Maintain attention, concentrate and move or stop quietly when appropriate (CL–LA)
* Initiate new combinations of movement and gesture to express and respond to feelings and ideas (EAD–BI)
* Notice changes in what is heard (CL–LA)
* Observe silences as part of a group, following agreed ideas and rules (PSED–MFB)
* Participate in a large group game or activity, understanding the need for rules and cooperation to ensure everybody's enjoyment (PSED–MR, MFB)
* Remember rules and aims of the game or activity and try various different strategies (PSED–MR, MFB)
* Select and use technology for particular purposes (UW–T)
* Construct with a purpose in mind, using a variety of resources (EAD–EUMM)
* Understand that different media can be combined to create new effects (EAD–EUMM)
* Use skills to explore concepts and ideas through representations (EAD–EUMM)

Octopus's garden

Themes
* Creatures/Animals/Birds/Plants
* Travelling/Places

Skills
* Movement/Dance
* Singing
* Acting/Mime
* Group work
* Craftwork

Equipment/Resources
A clear space with a safe, clean floor or ground surface; cardboard boxes, tissue boxes or shoe boxes; coloured papers and craft pieces for decoration; thin thread or elastic; coloured pens, pencils or crayons and scissors

Activity
Discuss with the children the types of creatures that live in the ocean and what they are like. Adapt a suitable song to fit an ocean theme. Walking Through the Jungle works well as: Swimming through the ocean, what do you see? If you hear a noise, what could it be?

Encourage children to pretend to be fish and to 'swim' freely around the space, avoiding each other, while singing or chanting the song in unison. After each chorus, invite a child to choose a creature and ask everybody to mime its movements and symbolic actions, such as the snapping jaws of a crocodile or a shaking motion for a jellyfish.

Invite two children to be an octopus, by standing back to back and linking elbows so that they have four legs and four arms – eight limbs between them. Ask the octopus to chase the fish, waving its arms, and try to touch them, while the fish dodge and try to avoid being caught. The first fish to be caught should freeze on the spot. The second fish to be caught can join up with the first fish to make an octopus. The first octopus can then become two fish and swim away again. The game can be as long or as short as the players wish. You could continue until all have had a turn at being an octopus, or allow more than one octopus at a time.

Extensions/Variations
Make creative models of undersea scenes with the children. Use a long tissue box that already has a hole in one side, or cut a rectangular or an oval hole in any cardboard box or use a shoe box without its lid.

Encourage the children to draw, decorate and cut out fish and sea creatures of various sizes. Hang them at different levels by attaching longer and shorter pieces of thread or elastic to them with sticky tape and sticking them to the inside of the top of the box.

Decorate the bottom and the back of the box by drawing and sticking on rocks, plants, shells, starfish, treasure chests, or whatever the children choose.

Learning objectives/Early Learning Goals
* Negotiate space successfully within a group, adjusting speed or changing direction to avoid obstacles or collisions (PD–MH)
* Portray different characters through a variety of movements and actions (EAD–BI)
* Make up simple songs and rhythms and adapt familiar ones to fit particular themes (EAD–BI)
* Share ideas within a group and develop imagination around a theme, showing sensitivity to others' needs and feelings and forming positive relationships (PSED-MR)
* Participate in a large group game or activity, understanding the need for rules and cooperation to ensure everybody's enjoyment (PSED–MR, MFB)
* Construct with a purpose in mind, using a variety of resources (EAD–EUMM)
* Safely use and explore a variety of materials, tools and techniques, experimenting with colour, design, texture, form and function (EAD–EUMM)
* Work cooperatively, taking turns to use equipment and sharing resources (PSED–MR)

Little bird

Themes
* Creatures/Animals/Birds/Plants
* Music/Sound

Skills
* Movement/Dance
* Acting/Mime
* Listening
* Confidence

Equipment/Resources
A safe, clear space in which children may move around easily; CD player; CD featuring some music or a song to suit a bird flying

Activity
Talk about birds and what they are like, where they live and what they eat. Encourage children to describe wings and flying, nests, eggs, worms, etc.

Invite children to pretend to be baby birds. Play some suitable music and mime with them. Sit inside a nest, feel hungry, look out of the nest, climb up to balance on the edge, jump off, flap your wings and fly away. Look down as you fly, spot a worm on the ground, fly down and peck it up with your beak, then fly away again. Repeat this sequence a few times, then fly back to the nest, land in it and curl up to go to sleep with your head under your wing. Encourage children to imitate your actions and to add their own ideas.

Use a song or piece of music that you are familiar with and adjust your mimed sequence to fit exactly. The bird should be just waking up as the music begins and falling asleep as it ends. Certain parts may sound more like flying, while other parts may indicate landing or feeding. Encourage the children to listen carefully and offer their suggestions and opinions by saying what particular parts of the music make them think of.

Extensions/Variations
Suggest that children pretend to be mother and father birds flying out to find food and bringing it back to feed their hungry baby birds in the nest.

Create mimed sequences in which other birds or animals search for food for themselves or their babies. Try owls, robins, squirrels, foxes or hedgehogs.

Provide a CD player and demonstrate how to use it safely, so that children may choose music and songs for themselves and create mimes during free play sessions.

Learning objectives/Early Learning Goals
* Listen carefully and imitate and create movement in response to types of music (EAD–EUMM, BI)
* Communicate meaning and express feelings through movement, mime and dance in various styles (EAD–BI)
* Develop good control and coordination in large and small movements (PD–MH)
* Match movements and actions to the space available (PD–MH)
* Negotiate space successfully within a group, adjusting speed or changing direction to avoid obstacles or collisions (PD–MH)
* Create simple representations of events and creatures to develop a watchable movement sequence within the boundaries of a given storyline or narrative (EAD–BI)
* Operate simple technological equipment to allow repeated listening to songs, music or sounds (UW–T)
* Think independently and offer ideas and opinions confidently to a group (PSED–SCSA; CL–S)

Move and freeze

Themes
* Ourselves/Bodies/Families
* Seasons/Weather/Elements
* Music/Sound

Skills
* Movement/Dance
* Listening
* Group work
* Acting/Mime
* Singing

Equipment/Resources
A safe, clear floor space in which children can move around easily; music player; song(s): We've Grown so Tall and/or Shaker Song (available to download from Brilliant Publications' website); CD player and CDs featuring suitable dance music; dressing-up costume items, accessories and props for dance and movement

Activity
Invite children to participate in a group movement game. Talk about all the different types of movements that we can make with our bodies and which parts of the body we use and move the most. Share a warm up song, such as We've Grown so Tall or Shaker Song. Play some popular dance music and encourage them to use all of the space, creating their own movements but negotiating safely around each other. (Adults should join in to model new steps and moves and be vigilant to avert potential collisions between children.)

Stop the music at frequent intervals and encourage all players to stop and imitate the adult leading the game, who might sit down quickly, freeze on the spot, balance on one leg, curl up very small, stretch out very wide or reach up very tall, etc. Start the music again after about five seconds and encourage everyone to move and dance again, until the next time it stops. (All children and adults play throughout the game – no one is asked to be 'out'.)

Talk about different seasons, temperatures and weather. Pretend to be holding umbrellas and skipping over or splashing in puddles while dancing, or include putting on or taking off warm jackets or scarves when the music stops, or balancing while wearing a sun hat.

Extensions/Variations
Teach children the names of all the movements they make while dancing and using the space (eg jumping, hopping, stepping, sliding, marching and swaying), then suggest that everyone tries to perform them as they are called out in turn.

Offer props to enhance dance and movement and improve spatial awareness, such as hoops or ribbons on sticks.

Encourage children to dance or move as different characters (eg older/younger people, tired/energetic people, quiet/noisy people) or as animals.

Learning objectives/Early Learning Goals
* Imitate and create movement and dance in response to music (EAD–EUMM, BI)
* Move freely and with pleasure and confidence in a range of ways (PD–MH)
* Negotiate space successfully, adjusting speed or changing direction to avoid obstacles or collisions (PD–MH)
* Maintain attention, concentrate and move or stop quietly when appropriate (CL–LA)
* Manage own basic personal needs successfully (PD–HSC)
* Notice changes in what is heard (CL–LA)
* Participate in a large group game or activity, understanding the need for rules and cooperation to ensure everybody's enjoyment ((PSED–MR, MFB)
* Portray characters and emotions through mime and expressive movement, understanding that the body can be used for communication (EAD–BI)
* Add to a growing repertoire of songs to be used in a variety of activities (EAD–EUMM)

Stand up, sit down

Themes
* Ourselves/Bodies/Families
* Music/Sound

Skills
* Movement/Dance
* Speech
* Confidence
* Singing
* Group work

Equipment/Resources
A safe, clear floor space in which adults and children can sit and stand comfortably in a group or a circle; music player; song: Shake 'n' Rattle (available to download from Brilliant Publications' website)

Activity
Gather children together and encourage them to think of different sounds and movements that they can make with their bodies while sitting down, such as clapping hands, stamping feet, clicking fingers, nodding or shaking heads, shutting eyes, tapping knees, touching shoulders and folding arms. Share a warm up song, such as Shake 'n' Rattle.

Encourage them to practise standing up and immediately sitting down again on the same spot. When working with older children, demonstrate how to do this neatly by moving smoothly from a kneeling position to a standing one and back again without putting any hands on the floor. (Rock forward slightly on the knees and then back onto the feet and straighten the knees to stand up; bend the knees to go down, rock forward to a kneeling position, lifting the feet slightly, then sit back on the feet.)

Chant in unison, as an example:
> Clap your hands, everyone together.
> Clap your hands, does it make a sound?
> Clap your hands, now be very clever.
> Clap your hands, stand up, sit down!

Perform the appropriate actions as you chant them, standing up and sitting down quickly.

Play the game for as long as the children's interest lasts, substituting different movements each time. For example: Shake your head, Stamp your feet and Wave your arms.

Extensions/Variations
Invite children to choose four movements to put together for one verse and to chant them and perform the actions quickly. For example: Stamp your feet, everyone together. Tap your knees, does it make a sound? Fold your arms, now be very clever. Click your fingers, stand up, sit down! Very few young children can actually 'click' their fingers and produce a sound, but they usually embrace the challenge and enjoy trying.

Discuss which actions produce sounds and which are silent, then combine them separately from the two groups to create noisy verses and quiet verses.

Learning objectives/Early Learning Goals
* Match movements and actions to the space available (PD–MH)
* Develop good control and coordination in large and small movements (PD–MH)
* Speak clearly in unison (CL–S; PSED–SCSA)
* Join in with repeated refrains and key events and phrases in rhymes and songs (CL–LA)
* Develop and use skills and explore concepts and ideas, embracing challenge and greater stimulation (EAD–BI)
* Follow instructions involving several ideas or actions (CL–U)
* Add to a growing repertoire of songs to be used in a variety of activities (EAD–EUMM)
* Participate in a large group game or activity, understanding the need for rules and cooperation to ensure everybody's enjoyment (PSED–MR, MFB)

Munching mini-beasts

Themes
* Food/Drinks/Meals
* Creatures/Animals/Birds/Plants
* Colours/Shapes/Numbers

Skills
* Movement/Dance
* Speech
* Group work
* Acting/Mime
* Confidence

Equipment/Resources
A clear space to work in with a safe, clean floor or ground surface; picture book – *The Very Hungry Caterpillar* by Eric Carle (Puffin); tape recorder and blank tape (or other recording device); magnifying glasses

Activity
Gather the group together and discuss how caterpillars, worms, slugs, snails and grubs move and feed. Encourage children to pretend to be these creatures and to crawl and slide along the floor. Talk about what they like to eat – fruit, vegetables, leaves – and the colours and shapes of the different foods.

Invite some practitioners and children to pretend to be the foods. Ask them to use their bodies to make arches and tunnels for others to wriggle through, by bending over forwards or backwards and standing on hands and feet. Invite the others to be caterpillars and other creatures and to crawl, slide and wriggle through the arches, miming that they are munching their way through apples, lettuce, etc.

Try arranging the foods in lines, then in circles and then scattered in spaces and challenge the children to follow the trails and move through as many as possible. Swap parts, so that all children have the opportunity to be both creatures and foods.

Extensions/Variations
Teach the children how to move like caterpillars that bunch up their bodies and then stretch them out again. (Adults beware – this is exhausting and can only be demonstrated for a short time!)

Read the story *The Very Hungry Caterpillar* and then invite groups of children to act it out simultaneously, performing as caterpillars and the right numbers of each piece of food. At the end, suggest that they all turn into butterflies and fly away around the room, then land on leaves to sleep. Provide a recording device and invite children to record their own voices as they re-tell the story and create sound effects.

Look for caterpillars, worms and other mini-beasts in the outdoor area. Use magnifying glasses to investigate their colours, shapes, patterns and count their legs.

Learning objectives/Early Learning Goals
* Portray different characters through a variety of movements and actions (EAD–BI)
* Match movements and actions to the space available (PD–MH)
* Use language to imagine and recreate ideas and experiences for acting and role-play (CL–S)
* Select and use technology for particular purposes (UW–T)
* Follow treasure hunts or trails in character, exploring an outdoor or indoor area as an animal or person from a story (UW–W; EAD–EUMM)
* Create simple representations of events, people, creatures or objects to develop a watchable movement sequence within the boundaries of a given storyline or narrative (EAD–BI)
* Understand a new concept and verbalize thinking and understanding (CL–U, S)

One brick at a time

Themes
* Building/Homes
* Seasons/Weather/Elements
* Music/Sound

Skills
* Movement/Dance
* Acting/Mime
* Speech
* Listening

Equipment/Resources
A clear space, with a safe, clean floor or ground surface, in which adults and children may move around or stand together comfortably in lines; large construction blocks, made from plastic, foam or wood; CD player; CD featuring suitable music or songs with steady beats and rhythms (One Brick At A Time and other songs from the musical stage show Barnum are ideal.)

Activity
Invite the children to make a pretend wall. Model picking up bricks and stacking them. Exaggerate how heavy they are and how much cement you need. Make the wall very high and catch any wobbly bricks that fall. Fetch a ladder and climb up your wall. Walk along the top, wobbling and holding your arms outstretched for balance. Imagine that a cold wind is blowing or rain is falling, which makes it harder to walk without swaying and stopping. Concentrate hard and move carefully to keep your balance.

Pretend that it is just one brick wide and you must step carefully with one foot exactly in front of the other. Sit down to look at the view, lean back and 'fall' off the wall! Imagine that, luckily, you are a bird (or a mini-beast, fairy, pixie, dragon, dinosaur or superhero) with wings and fly up into the sky.

Ask children to stand in a line with a practitioner at each end. Establish a steady clapping rhythm of one clap each two seconds, turning the upper body to one side and then the other in time with the claps. Suggest that there is a pile of pretend bricks built into a tall tower at one end of the line and invite the children to help to move the tower to the other end, one brick at a time. Ask the adult to take a pretend brick from the tower and pass it to the child beside them in the line. Each person in the line should then pass bricks from the player on one side to the player on the other side, while the adult at the end re-builds the tower as each brick is received. Play music with a suitable beat and rhythm and pass bricks steadily. Play music with a faster beat and ask players to pass bricks more quickly, to keep in time.

Extensions/Variations
Ask children to describe how heavy the bricks were (as an elephant or a car), what they used to stick them together (cement – or glue, sticky tape, honey, treacle or syrup), how high their walls were (as high as a castle or a crane), what they could see from the top (clouds, sun, rainbow, sheep, roads, rivers, cars – or dinosaurs, jungles or space) and which winged creature they pretended to be. Encourage children to listen to each other as they take their turns to speak, and to think of fantasy worlds and funny ideas alongside more serious ones.

Try using real blocks and building real towers, while still exaggerating the movements to pass, receive and place bricks dramatically.

Learning objectives/Early Learning Goals
* Interact as a member of a group to develop and act out a narrative (EAD–BI)
* Move rhythmically and show awareness of tempo and mood (EAD–EUMM)
* Develop good control and coordination in large and small movements (PD–MH)
* Share ideas within a group and develop imagination around a theme, showing sensitivity to others' needs and feelings and forming positive relationships (PSED–MR)
* Use language to imagine and recreate ideas and experiences for acting and role play (CL–S)
* Speak confidently within a familiar group to describe an activity (PSED–SCSA)
* Copy and tap out simple repeated rhythms (EAD–EUMM)

Contrasts

Themes
* Music/Sound
* Creatures/Animals/Birds/Plants

Skills
* Movement/Dance
* Acting/Mime
* Listening
* Confidence

Equipment/Resources
A safe, clear space in which children can move around each other easily; tambourine and other percussion instruments; music player; instrumental track: The Wheels on the Bus (available to download from Brilliant Publications' website)

Activity
Play a tambourine for the children to listen to. First, bang it firmly and suggest that it sounds like a kangaroo jumping. Next tap it more gently, with a 'one, two' beat and say that it reminds you of a horse trotting. Lastly, shake it and suggest that it sounds like a rattle snake wriggling along the ground.

Invite the children to make the appropriate movements when they hear the sounds. Play one type of beat after another, in a random order, so that they can act out each of the three creatures several times.

At intervals, hold the tambourine still for a few seconds. Ask the children to freeze silently when there is no sound and to listen carefully for the next tambourine cue.

Extensions/Variations
Ask children to match the speed of their movements to the sounds as they are played. Gradually tap or shake more and more quickly, until all of the children are making very fast movements, then gradually slow down again, playing more and more slowly until the children are hardly moving.

Try using other instruments and asking the children to say what they think they sound like and to suggest creatures to act out and their movements.

Welcome all of the children's ideas and tell them that they don't only have to think of living creatures. They may mention, for example, plants growing, trees blowing in the wind, cars driving or thunderstorms.

Invite children to choose instrument sounds to enhance the singing and performance of a well known song, such as The Wheels on the Bus.

Learning objectives/Early Learning Goals
* Listen carefully and imitate and create movement in response to types of music (EAD–EUMM, BI)
* Communicate meaning and express feelings through movement and mime (EAD–BI)
* Maintain attention, concentrate and move or stop quietly when appropriate (CL–LA)
* Negotiate space successfully within a group, adjusting speed or changing direction to avoid obstacles or collisions (PD–MH)
* Portray characters and emotions through mime and expressive movement, understanding that the body can be used for communication (EAD–BI)
* Notice changes in what is heard (CL–LA)
* Observe silences as part of a group, following agreed ideas and rules (PSED–MFB)
* Explore the different sounds of instruments and use them appropriately to enhance performances (EAD–EUMM)
* Improve confidence and social skills through participation in a large group activity (PSED–MR, MFB; PD–MH)

A turn to dance

Themes
* Music/Sound
* Ourselves/Bodies/Families
* Times of Year/Celebrations

Skills
* Movement/Dance
* Acting/Mime
* Listening
* Confidence

Equipment/Resources
A clear space in which adults and children can talk, work and move together safely and comfortably in small groups; music player; songs: Your Shoes and Click Your Fingers (available to download from Brilliant Publications' website); CD player and CDs featuring popular children's songs or dance music; curtain or blanket, string and lamps

Activity
Invite children to form small groups of 3–6 who will create a dance together to show to everybody else. Allot a practitioner to each group or small number of groups, to supervise, advise and support. Give the children ideas of basic steps and moves by sharing songs such as Your Shoes and Click Your Fingers.

Ask the children to sit and listen while you play a short chosen song or piece of music through once. Allow them a little time to talk and discuss ideas, then play the music again and invite them to practise steps and movements together until all groups are ready.

Provide a stage area, using stage blocks or fabric or chalk lines on the floor. Rig a 'house tab' by hanging a curtain or blanket over a string tied across the room and/or turn on lamps and direct them towards the stage area. Invite the groups to perform to each other in turn. Remind them to bow at the end of their dances and to clap each other. Praise them all highly for effort, originality and teamwork, picking out different specific areas for extra praise for each group, such as the number or speed of moves, careful balancing, remembering a routine or helping each other. If the children are old enough, introduce the idea of constructive criticism by asking whether anybody can suggest how to make a routine even better. Comment on how different group dances look, even when they sound the same.

Extensions/Variations
Provide percussion instruments that children can shake or tap as they move around and invite them to include sounds within their dance routines. (Avoid those played in the mouth unless children will be seated while playing them, in case they trip or collide while dancing.)

Suggest that some children might play instruments while others dance to the sounds. This idea could be developed by individual groups, or groups could play for each other's dances. Support the children in preparing and practising music and dances for end of term events and special occasions. Invite parents and carers into the setting regularly to watch the performances.

Learning objectives/Early Learning Goals
* Listen carefully and imitate and create movement in response to types of music (EAD–EUMM, BI)
* Move rhythmically and show awareness of tempo and mood (EAD–EUMM)
* Explore and learn how sounds can be changed (EAD–EUMM)
* Memorize simple dances and confidently perform them to others, individually or within a group (EAD–EUMM; PSED–SCSA)
* Thank an audience after a performance, through body language (EAD–BI)
* Explore the different sounds of instruments and use them appropriately to enhance performances (EAD–EUMM)
* Work, speak and listen appropriately as a member of a group, showing sensitivity to others' needs and feelings and responding with consideration (PSED–MR)

Over the river

Themes
* Travelling/Places
* Seasons/Weather/Elements

Skills
* Movement/Dance
* Acting/Mime
* Confidence
* Singing

Equipment/Resources
A clear space in which children may move around, with a safe, clean floor or ground surface; a quantity of cushions, mats, hoops, sacks or foam squares – or playground chalk

Activity
Scatter the cushions or similar items in a wavy line across the floor area, or draw circles or squares on the ground outside with chalk.

Tell the children that they are stepping stones to help them to cross the river. Model stepping or jumping from one to another and invite the children to follow you.

Encourage mimes and acting, such as raising knees high to exaggerate steps, balancing on one leg, slipping and sliding or wobbling as you step and, at some point, pretend to lose your balance and 'fall into the river'.

Ask the children to 'fall in' too and to choose whether to climb out again, or swim to the shore, or turn into a river creature.

Suggest that the children pretend to row boats all around the space, either individually or as pairs or small groups rowing in unison, then to capsize and fall dramatically into the water.

They might then choose to act out a scenario that involves swimming away from a shark or a crocodile, or they might like to turn into sharks or crocodiles and chase the adults!

Extensions/Variations
Play similar games involving going over the mountain, over the hot, sandy desert or over the swamp in the jungle or forest.

Sing appropriate songs while enjoying the activity, such as: The Bear Went Over the Mountain and Row, Row, Row Your Boat.

Gradually move the stepping stones a little further apart or make the wavy trail harder to follow, to challenge children's acting, balance and thinking skills.

Imagine extra challenges, such as crossing while the wind is blowing strongly or balancing while the stones are slippery with rain.

Learning objectives/Early Learning Goals
* Initiate new combinations of movement and gesture to express and respond to feelings and ideas (EAD–BI)
* Portray different characters through a variety of movements and actions (EAD–BI)
* Develop good control and coordination in large and small movements (PD–MH)
* Develop and act out an experience, a storyline or a narrative, working cooperatively within a group, and practise skills to perform before others with confidence (EAD–BI; PSED–SCSA)
* Create simple representations of events, people, creatures or objects to develop a watchable movement sequence within the boundaries of a given storyline or narrative (EAD–BI)
* Improve confidence and social skills through participation in a large group activity (PSED–MR, MFB; PD–MH)
* Memorize simple songs, including words, tunes and appropriate actions, and sing them in unison with others, maintaining a steady speed and volume (EAD–EUMM)

© Debbie Chalmers and Brilliant Publications

Up the hill

Themes
* Travelling/Places
* Nursery Rhymes/Poems/Songs

Skills
* Movement/Dance
* Acting/Mime
* Singing
* Speech
* Craftwork

Equipment/Resources
A safe, clear space in which children can move around each other easily; music player; song: The Train (available to download from Brilliant Publications' website); calendar of pictures or photographs of hills and mountains; white paper; paints, crayons or pastels and pencils

Activity
Create a symbolic hill by placing a large beanbag or a pile of cushions in the middle of the floor. Imagine that it is very steep and very high. Lead the group in miming the climbing of the hill. Lift legs and knees high, mime tiredness and concentration and use a rope to haul yourself up. After the mime, introduce new vocabulary by talking about pulling, pushing, crawling, staggering, lurching and pausing, feeling weary, exhausted, excited and amazed.

Reach the top and stand still to look at the view, then choose whether to climb down carefully, stepping backwards and holding onto the rope; or to run, slide or roll down quickly. Invite each person to say what they saw from the top. Remember that mime can be fantasy and answers could range from clouds, aeroplanes and rainbows to tractors in fields, dinosaurs and flying pigs! Accept all ideas and show interest in each child's comments. Encourage all children to listen to each other.

Extensions/Variations
Sing the song She'll Be Coming Round the Mountain When She Comes while dancing around the beanbag and perform appropriate actions. Sing or chant nursery rhymes involving climbing hills, such as Jack and Jill and The Grand Old Duke of York, and create actions and mimes. Pretend to ride in a train to climb a hill, singing along with songs such as The Train or Train-Is-A-Coming, making arm movements in a 'follow the leader' line.

Read stories and non-fiction books about animals and explorers climbing mountains.

Ask children to study the calendar pictures and then paint or draw their own. Make a display of all the pictures and add appropriate labels and captions. Invite children to make these with you and encourage them all to attempt to write, copy or trace over their names.

Learning objectives/Early Learning Goals
* Initiate new combinations of movement and gesture to express feelings and ideas (EAD–BI)
* Learn and use the vocabulary of movement and controlled effort (PD–MH)
* Develop and act out an experience, a storyline or a narrative, working cooperatively within a group (EAD–BI; PSED–SCSA)
* Memorize simple songs, including words, tunes and appropriate actions, and sing them in unison with others, maintaining a steady speed and volume (EAD–EUMM)
* Use language to imagine and recreate ideas and experiences for acting and role-play (CL–S)
* Talk about and explain the symbolic use of furniture and objects in pretend situations (CL–S)
* Use skills to explore concepts and ideas through representations (EAD–EUMM)
* Capture experiences and responses with a range of media (EAD–BI)
* Write own name and labels and captions (L–W)
* Handle equipment and tools effectively, including pencils for drawing and writing (PD–MH)

Puddle jumping

Themes
* Seasons/Weather/Elements
* Creatures/Animals/ Birds/Plants

Skills
* Movement/Dance
* Singing

Equipment/Resources
A clear, safe space, both indoors and outdoors; music player; songs: We've Grown so Tall and Umbrella; instrumental track: Five Little Speckled Frogs (songs and instrumental track available to download from Brilliant Publications' website); a wet day, which has created puddles in the outdoor area; coats, boots and umbrellas for adults and children

Activity
Celebrate a wet day with this activity. Begin indoors with a discussion about rain. Encourage children to share their experiences of travelling to the setting through the rain and to look through the windows at the puddles forming outside.

Share the action songs We've Grown so Tall and Umbrella and encourage children to practise jumping over imaginary puddles.

Support the children in dressing appropriately for wet weather, then take them outside.

Encourage them to jump into puddles and from puddle to puddle, enjoying the splashes they make and noticing their wet footprints.

Ask the children to become ducks and to think of and demonstrate the movements that they make as they enjoy the rain. Repeat the activity as frogs.

Suggest appropriate songs to sing as they splash around, such as Five Little Ducks Went Swimming One Day or Five Little Speckled Frogs.

Extensions/Variations
Encourage children to help each other to put boots on the correct feet, fasten coats and find hats, scarves and gloves, rather than always waiting for an adult to help.

Support small groups of children in creating 'rain dances' by stepping, jumping and turning around the puddles and spinning their umbrellas and moving them up and down.

Learning objectives/Early Learning Goals
* Manage own personal needs successfully and offer help to others (PD–HSC)
* Move freely and with pleasure and confidence in a range of ways (PD–MH)
* Memorize simple dances and confidently perform them to others, individually or within a group (EAD–EUMM; PSED–SCSA)
* Portray characters and emotions through mime and expressive movement, understanding that the body can be used for communication (EAD–BI)
* Add to a growing repertoire of familiar songs and dances to be used in a variety of situations and activities (EAD–EUMM)
* Confidently use songs and rhymes that involve number names, counting on and counting back (M–N)

Musical hats

Themes
* Times of Year/Celebrations
* People Who Help Us/Occupations

Skills
* Movement/Dance
* Listening
* Group work
* Craftwork

Equipment/Resources
A clear space with a safe, clean floor surface, in which adults and children can sit comfortably in a circle; two or more hats/headdresses appropriate to the theme of the game – such as santa hat, elf hat and reindeer antlers or police officer cap and firefighter helmet; CD player; CD featuring seasonal music or children's songs; coloured card and paper, scissors, sticky tape, plastic hair bands

Activity
Explain that the game involves passing the hats around the circle while the music plays, with each person trying them on in turn. (Hats must be put on and taken off each head, not just passed from hand to hand.) Whenever the music stops, the people wearing or holding the hats must pass them to the next player and lie back on the floor. The hats are then passed over them in the next turn.

Ask one practitioner to operate the music, watching the players and being sensitive in choosing when to stop and restart it.

The game becomes more and more amusing as players have to stretch to reach each other, while the lying down players try to help or stay out of the way, and ends when the last players left sitting up are all wearing hats.

Extensions/Variations
Choose the music carefully and encourage trying to pass the hats in time to it, using slower songs for younger children and faster ones for older and more confident players. Add extra challenge by selecting a different track for each turn, choosing some faster and some slower songs, and asking children to play accordingly.

Use the same rules but vary the focus of the game, by providing other items of clothing to put on and take off, instruments to play, or soft toys to cuddle before passing them on.

Provide a simple CD player for the children and demonstrate its use, so that they may access it independently and play similar games without adults.

Support children in making hats and headdresses to their own designs. Cut pieces from coloured card and paper and attach them to each other and then to plastic hair bands, so that they can be worn by anyone. Small hats that stand straight up from the head look effective; try clowns' cone hats, top hats, crowns and tiaras, or make up your own crazy designs!

Learning objectives/Early Learning Goals
* Move rhythmically and show awareness of tempo and mood (EAD–EUMM)
* Maintain attention, concentrate and move or stop quietly when appropriate (CL–LA)
* Notice changes in what is heard (CL–LA)
* Observe silences as part of a group, following agreed ideas and rules (PSED–MFB)
* Operate simple technological equipment to allow repeated listening to songs, music, sounds or stories (UW–T)
* Participate in a large group game or activity, understanding the need for rules and cooperation to ensure everybody's enjoyment ((PSED–MR, MFB)
* Use available resources to create costume pieces and props to support role-play (EAD–BI)

Cross the bridge

Themes
* Stories/Fairy Tales
* Creatures/Animals/Birds/Plants
* Travelling/Places

Skills
* Movement/Dance
* Acting/Mime
* Speech
* Singing

Equipment/Resources
A clear space in which children may move around, with a safe, clean floor or ground surface; a version of the story: The Billy Goats Gruff; five or six hoops; green fabric or paper to symbolise grass – or a real grassy area if playing outside

Activity
Read the story The Billy Goats Gruff with the children.

Lay out hoops in a line with grass at one end.

Invite children to pretend to be the 'Billy Goats Gruff' and to cross the bridge to reach the green grass. Remind them to step carefully and quietly and to try not to disturb the troll.

As they take turns to step into the hoops, ask a practitioner to suddenly step into a hoop in front of them and make a scary face. Encourage the 'goats' to pretend to be frightened and to run back to the other end of the bridge to start again.

The 'troll' can gradually allow a few children past at a time before scaring the others, until they all reach the grass.

Extensions/Variations
Invite children to take turns to be the troll and make a scary face to send the goats back. Discuss which expressions are scary and good acting, and which are rude and not suitable for the game.

Encourage children to work in small groups to remember or make up suitable speeches for the goats and the troll, and to talk while acting out the story.

Pretend that the troll and the biggest billy goat were so heavy that they stamped holes in the bridge and made it fall down. Sing a suitable song, such as London Bridge, and create a mime sequence to rebuild it. (Tune available as an instrumental recording – track 30 on CD *J'aime Chanter* – Brilliant Publications.)

Learning objectives/Early Learning Goals
* Initiate new combinations of movement and gesture to express and respond to feelings and ideas (EAD–BI)
* Create simple representations of events, people, creatures or objects to develop a watchable movement sequence within the boundaries of a given storyline or narrative (EAD–BI)
* Explore and develop skills of characterization within a small group, using different forms of language and intonation to imagine and recreate roles and experiences (CL–S)
* Use language to imagine and recreate ideas and experiences for acting and role-play (CL–S)
* Take cues confidently to speak in character to continue a storyline (L–R)
* Add to a growing repertoire of familiar songs and dances to be used in a variety of situations and activities (EAD–EUMM)

Guess who I am

Themes
* People Who Help Us/Occupations
* Times of Year/Celebrations
* Stories/Fairy Tales
* Nursery Rhymes/Poems/Songs
* Creatures/Animals/Birds/Plants

Skills
* Acting/Mime
* Confidence
* Group work
* Speech

Equipment/Resources
A safe, clear space in which adults and children can sit or stand together comfortably in a group

Activity
Gather the group together and invite them to play a guessing game. Mime an animal, such as a cat or an elephant, and ask who can guess what it is. Explain that mime must be silent and people must guess from your actions, not by the sound the animal would make. Invite other practitioners and then children to take turns to mime different animals for the group to guess.

Repeat the activity with another theme, such as 'people who help us' or 'people from stories or songs'. Invite children to mime the actions of fire fighters, police officers, nurses, taxi drivers, hairdressers, etc. Alternatively, suggest that they mime as characters, such as the wolf blowing a house down, Jack climbing the beanstalk, a wicked witch or wizard, Humpty Dumpty falling off a wall, blind mice or Incy Wincy Spider. Make the game seasonal or appropriate for any special occasion by miming appropriate characters or objects, such as Father Christmas, reindeer, robins, crackers, bells and donkeys.

Mime actions and occupations instead and ask the group if they can guess what each person is doing, such as sawing wood, answering the telephone, writing, singing, dancing or reading a book.

Extensions/Variations
Invite children to form pairs or small groups and think of a mime together, then practise and perform it for the rest of the group to guess. Practitioners may need to quietly offer some ideas or suggestions at first, such as playing a game of snap, taking turns to push each other on a swing or taking a dog for a walk.

Offer a general theme and ask each person to independently think of a mime related to it. Inevitably, some people will think of the same idea, but all the mimes will be different. For example, a seaside theme could lead to mimes as varied as sailing boats, swimming, paddling, digging sand castles, eating ice creams, holding up umbrellas and being crabs and jellyfish.

Learning objectives/Early Learning Goals
* Re-enact real, first-hand experiences through imaginative role-play (EAD–BI)
* Portray characters and emotions through mime and expressive movement, understanding that the body can be used for communication (EAD–BI)
* Develop and use skills and explore concepts and ideas, embracing challenge and greater stimulation (EAD–BI)
* Participate in a large group game or activity, understanding the need for rules and cooperation to ensure everybody's enjoyment (PSED–MR, MFB)
* Remember the rules and aims of the game or activity and try various different strategies (PSED–MR, MFB)
* Use talk to organize, sequence and clarify thinking, ideas, feelings and events when planning scenarios or performances (CL–S)

Make a machine

Themes
* People Who Help Us/Occupations
* Music/Sound
* Colours/Shapes/Numbers

Skills
* Acting/Mime
* Movement/Dance
* Speech
* Listening
* Confidence
* Craftwork

Equipment/Resources
A clear space in which adults and children can move around easily and safely; CD player; CDs featuring appropriate music or songs for robotic and machine actions; storybooks containing pictures of crazy machines by Dr Seuss (Random House, Inc.); storybooks about Bertha the Big Machine by Eric Charles and Steve Augarde (Hippo Books); found and recycled materials, coloured pens, scissors, glue and sticky tape.

Activity
Talk with the children about machines, who might use them and for what purposes. Focus on machines that make products or perform specific tasks, such as those in factories and on building sites. Find out whether any of the children's relations are factory workers, packers, builders, carpenters or crane or fork lift drivers. Discuss fictional robots and machines and read some stories about Bertha, the Big Machine. If possible, obtain some episodes on DVD (by Ivor Wood, Woodland Animations Ltd) or the songs on CD (Bryan Daly).

Play appropriate music and invite everybody to practise making jerky, robotic movements with arms, legs and head while walking around the room. Then try standing still and making machine-type movements with the whole body on the spot.

Ask children to stand in a long line and pretend that they are the separate parts of one large machine. Pass a pretend box to the first child in the line and ask for each person to use their robotic arms to pass it all the way along to another practitioner at the other end. Then start again with a pretend product, such as a jigsaw puzzle, make up a simple story about how it is made and ask each person in the machine to work on it in a different way as it is passed along the line. For example, different people might paint a picture, cut it into pieces, count the pieces, fit some together, scoop them into a box, close the box and stick a picture onto it. Encourage the children to count how many puzzles they make and pretend to stack them in a very tall pile.

Extensions/Variations
Support children in creating machines within small groups. They could choose music, make up movements and actions and describe and show what their machine does or makes.

Read some Dr Seuss books that feature crazy machines and make them available in the book area so that children may return to look at the pictures independently. Discuss the different colours and shapes of the machines and count how many wheels, cogs, etc they have. Provide found and recycled materials for junk modelling in a variety of colours and shapes and encourage children to design and make their own machines.

Learning objectives/Early Learning Goals
* Work cooperatively with others to act out a familiar part of a storyline (EAD–BI)
* Create simple representations of events, people or objects to develop a watchable movement sequence within the boundaries of a given storyline or narrative (EAD–BI)
* Develop good control in large and small movements (PD–MH)
* Use language to imagine and recreate ideas and experiences for acting and role-play (CL–S)
* Explain own knowledge and understanding, ask appropriate questions of others, take account of others' ideas and resolve conflicts through compromise (PSED–MR)
* Operate simple technological equipment to allow listening to songs, music or sounds (UW–T)
* Understand a new concept and verbalize thinking and understanding (CL–U, S)
* Use media and materials in original ways to suit different uses or purposes (EAD–BI)

Make a face

Themes
* Ourselves/Bodies/Families
* Nursery Rhymes/Poems/Songs

Skills
* Acting/Mime
* Confidence

Equipment/Resources
A quiet place for a group of adults and children to sit, free from distractions; music player; instrumental track: If You've Happy and You Know it (available to download from Brilliant Publications' website)

Activity
Invite children to practise miming, explaining that mime is acting without any sounds or talking. Show them a collection of familiar facial expressions and invite them to imitate each one (eg happy, sad, cross, tired, excited, surprised, worried, thinking), telling them what they are called. Use pictures, photographs or posters, or just demonstrate with your own face.

Make expressions in turn and ask the group of children to copy them and then to name them. Invite children to take turns to lead by choosing and making an expression for the group to copy and guess.

Discuss different expressions with the children, when the miming is over, and how they show people's feelings. Encourage them to talk about how different behaviours can affect the ways people feel, such as when friends are cross because someone forgets to share or when parents are pleased because their child does something kind. Help them to understand that their own expressions can show their feelings (so they should smile and look friendly when they want others to play with them), and that they can use other people's expressions as clues to tell when they are happy, sad, cross or worried (in order to comfort a friend or to stop doing something that is starting to annoy a family member).

Play a rapid game involving an adult calling out 'Who can make the crossest face?' or 'Who can make the most excited face?' etc. Challenge children to 'keep up' and to make each expression before the next one is called out.

Extensions/Variations
Suggest that children sit in a circle and pass an expression around, taking turns to choose and make a face and show it to the person on their right, who copies the face for their neighbour, until it comes back to the first person. Praise the group when they manage to keep the same face all around the circle. Discourage silly or rude faces, but allow 'fierce' or 'scary' if they are well prepared.

Invite children to sit in two long lines, facing each other, and to take turns to make expressions and to be the 'mirrors' who copy them.

Share songs and rhymes that describe various emotions and encourage children to use different expressions while singing or saying them. Try: If You're Happy and You Know it, How Do You Feel Today?, Clap Your Hands, Little Miss Muffet and Hey Diddle Diddle.

Learning objectives/Early Learning Goals
* Confidently try a new activity and explore an unfamiliar theme (PSED–SCSA)
* Portray characters and emotions through mime and expressions, understanding that the face and body can be used to communicate meaning (EAD–BI)
* Improve confidence and social skills through participation in a large group activity (PSED–MR, MFB; PD–MH)
* Develop and use skills and explore concepts and ideas, embracing challenge and greater stimulation (EAD–BI)

Raiding the nest

Themes
* Ourselves/Bodies/Families
* Creatures/Animals/Birds/Plants

Skills
* Acting/Mime
* Listening
* Group work

Equipment/Resources
A safe, clear space in which adults and children may sit comfortably in a circle; a quantity of eggs (toy or craft or hard boiled) or foam balls or similar (or shiny objects, carrots, jewellery, maracas or bells, etc)

Activity
First, encourage the children to practise making quiet creeping movements, then loud clapping and stamping movements. Also discuss and practise a range of facial expressions. Talk about maintaining control of the body through concentration and practise freezing in silence.

Invite the children to sit in a circle with a practitioner sitting in the middle, to be a mother or father bird in its nest. Make a pile of eggs beside the bird. Use toy eggs made of plastic, rubber or wood or paper-spun craft eggs or hard boiled eggs, foam balls or anything similar.

While the bird pretends to sleep in the nest, silently point to two or three children who then creep to the nest, take an egg, creep back and hide it behind them. Encourage everybody to stay absolutely silent during this movement.

Ask everybody to clap their hands or stamp their feet to wake up the bird, who will then try to guess who has taken the eggs. Encourage the children now to make lots of different expressions (happy, sad, cross, worried, surprised, etc) to hide any guilty faces and confuse the bird. When the bird guesses where the missing eggs are, they are returned to their family in the nest.

Extensions/Variations
Make lots of smaller circles and invite children to take turns to be the birds.

Vary this game to suit any theme. There could be a dragon guarding a nest of jewels, a rabbit with carrots hidden in a burrow, or a pirate sleeping beside a treasure chest, etc.

To increase concentration and make the game more challenging, use noisy objects, such as maracas, bells, rustling paper or a bunch of keys, to make it harder to steal the objects secretly.

Learning objectives/Early Learning Goals
* Portray characters and emotions through mime and expressive movement, understanding that the body can be used for communication (EAD–BI)
* Maintain concentration in a large group activity and cooperate in a game that requires turn taking and understanding of rules (PSED–MR, MFB)
* Observe silences as part of a group, following agreed ideas and rules (PSED–MFB)
* Remember rules and aims of the game or activity and try various different strategies (PSED–MR, MFB)

Dig a hole

Themes
* Building/Homes
* Travelling/Places
* Seasons/Weather/Elements

Skills
* Acting/Mime
* Movement/Dance
* Speech
* Confidence
* Singing

Equipment/Resources
A clear space with a safe, clean floor surface, in which adults and children can move around easily and sit comfortably; music player; songs: Windows, The Train and/or Aeroplane (available to download from Brilliant Publications' website)

Activity
Invite children to join you in the pretend train which is going to the seaside. Mime buying a ticket, waiting at the station, getting into the train, bouncing along and looking out of the windows. Express excitement that you have arrived when the train stops and climb out carefully, wave goodbye and run down to the beach. Model digging holes and building sand castles on the beach and encourage the children to copy you. After a short while, lead them in miming the digging of big, deep holes, pretending that it is starting to rain, putting up umbrellas, jumping into their holes to shelter from the rain and sitting down to look around. Talk about dropping things and losing them in sand.

Encourage each child in turn to hold up a pretend item that he has found in his hole and to show the group what it is using mime. Practitioners could take the first turns, to ensure that the children understand. Ask all children to watch each other quietly and try to guess.

Simple examples that are easy to act out might be: a bouncing ball, a skipping rope, a kite, a pair of boots, an umbrella, a banana, a car or a dog (they don't have to be sensible or realistic). If children choose mimes that are harder to guess, ask if they can give any verbal clues to help their audience.

Extensions/Variations
Lead the whole group in building a pretend sand castle together in the middle of the floor, then digging a moat around it and filling it with buckets of water fetched from the sea.

Invite children to pretend to dig sand and build up mounds, then climb up to stand on top and say what the weather is like and what they can see.

Suggest that you might travel in an aeroplane instead of a train and go to a beach in another country. Ask the children if they have any experiences of family holidays abroad, in hot or cold places, to share and create appropriate mime sequences together. Set the sequences to music chosen by practitioners or children, or use the songs: Windows, The Train and/or Aeroplane.

Learning objectives/Early Learning Goals
* Re-enact real, first-hand experiences through imaginative role play (EAD–BI)
* Create simple representations of events, creatures, people or objects to develop a watchable movement sequence within the boundaries of a given storyline or narrative (EAD–BI)
* Maintain concentration and participation in a large group activity and cooperate in a game that requires turn taking and understanding of rules (PSED–MR, MFB)
* Initiate new combinations of movement and gesture to express and respond to feelings and ideas (EAD–BI)
* Speak confidently within a familiar group and take turns to initiate discussion, describe an activity or perform a speech, song or rhyme, asking for help if needed (PSED–SCSA)
* Work, speak and listen appropriately as a member of a group, showing sensitivity to others' needs and feelings and responding with consideration (PSED–MR)
* Add to a growing repertoire of familiar songs and dances to be used in a variety of situations and activities (EAD–EUMM)

Welcome to my home

Themes
* Building/Homes
* Seasons/Weather/Elements
* Creatures/Animals/Birds/Plants

Skills
* Acting/Mime
* Movement/Dance
* Speech
* Confidence
* Craftwork

Equipment/Resources
A large, clear, safe space in which adults and children can work together comfortably; blankets, rugs, sheets and large pieces of fabric; clothes pegs that snap open and shut; child-sized tables and chairs; computer and printer with paper; song: Windows (available to download from Brilliant Publications' website); Internet access; non-fiction picture books featuring animals and their homes

Activity
Invite children to make dens and homes to 'live in' with their friends and encourage them to form small groups, each with a supporting practitioner. Provide each group with one or more tables and two or more chairs, several blankets or similar and a number of clothes pegs. Ask them to discuss ideas and make plans, then work together to create a home big enough for them all, that will keep them cool in summer and warm and dry in winter.

Invite children to make welcome signs to put up outside the home doorways. Support each group in turn as they decide how to use the computer together to create words such as: Welcome to our house! or Come inside! and to add pictures and designs to the poster.

Encourage children to pretend to be animals living in dens, setts or burrows, such as foxes, badgers or rabbits. Ask them to act out scenes such as running out of their homes to look for food and bringing it back to eat it or to feed it to their babies.

Extensions/Variations
Suggest that groups take turns to visit each other's new homes and to see whether they can all squeeze inside together. Sing or chant the song Windows.

Gather the whole group back together and ask them to describe their new homes and the similarities and differences between them that they have discovered.

Talk about our need for shelter and how we would feel if we didn't have a home to keep us safe and protected from weather and extreme temperatures, especially at night times.

Use books and the Internet to research the different types of homes made and used by animals, birds and other creatures. Introduce nocturnal and nomadic creatures and those that live on plants. Mime the movements and feelings of these creatures.

Learning objectives/Early Learning Goals
* Share ideas within a group and develop imagination around a theme, showing sensitivity to others' needs and feelings and forming positive relationships (PSED–MR)
* Confidently try a new activity and explore an unfamiliar theme (PSED–SCSA)
* Develop good control and coordination in large and small movements (PD–MH)
* Use talk to organize, sequence and clarify thinking, ideas, feelings and events when planning scenarios or performances (CL–S)
* Understand a new concept and verbalize thinking and understanding (CL–U, S)
* Capture experiences and responses with a range of media (EAD–BI)
* Use a simple program on a computer to produce text, pictures and designs (UW–T)
* Use identifiable letters and phonic knowledge to communicate meaning (L–W)

The wind blows

Theme
* Seasons/Weather/Elements
* Ourselves/Bodies/Families
* Creatures/Animals/Birds/Plants

Skills
* Acting/Mime
* Movement/Dance
* Listening

Equipment/Resources
A safe, clear space in which children can move around easily – indoors and then outdoors; pocket kites; bubble mixture with wands and blowers; a windy day!

Activity
Beginning indoors, ask the children to imagine that it is a very windy day and that they are out for a walk. Model appropriate mimes and movements to show that you are struggling against the wind and pushing through it, as it tries to blow you back. Talk about the feeling of the wind and your movements through and against it, using descriptive vocabulary.

Suggest mimes such as: shivering with cold, pulling on gloves, hats and scarves, stamping feet in boots, catching or kicking falling leaves, flying kites or blowing bubbles and chasing after them.

Imagine with the children that you are birds soaring in the sky, catching the wind under your wings and gliding. Then imagine that you are a small animal huddling inside a nest or den, out of the wind.

Support children in dressing appropriately in outdoor clothes and shoes or boots, then take them outside to experience wind blowing.

Extensions/Variations
Encourage children to help each other to find, put on and fasten their outdoor clothes.

Play at shuffling through leaves, flying pocket kites and blowing bubbles out in the wind.

Listen to the sounds the wind makes and watch the trees moving. Pretend to be trees and mime the branches and leaves blowing in both strong and gentle winds.

Learning objectives/Early Learning Goals
* Re-enact real, first-hand experiences through imaginative role play (EAD–BI)
* Portray characters and emotions through mime and expressive movement, understanding that the body can be used for communication (EAD–BI)
* Create simple representations of events, people, creatures or objects to develop a watchable movement sequence within the boundaries of a given storyline or narrative (EAD–BI)
* Initiate new combinations of movement and gesture to express and respond to feelings and ideas (EAD–BI)
* Learn and use the vocabulary of movement and controlled effort (PD–MH)
* Manage own personal needs successfully and offer help to others (PD–HSC)
* Notice changes in what is heard (CL–LA)

Weather forecast

Themes
* Seasons/Weather/Elements
* Travelling/Places

Skills
* Acting/Mime
* Speech
* Listening

Equipment/Resources
A safe, clear space in which children can separate to work independently in pairs or small groups and then perform to each other

Activity
Ask the children to think about any weather forecasts that they have seen on television and to talk together about all the different types of weather that we have in this country.

Suggest that one of each pair or one or two of each group describe the weather, while the other(s) mime what they are saying. For example, when the announcers say that there will be rain, the actors could indicate falling raindrops with their fingers, pretend to splash in puddles and hold up imaginary umbrellas.

Some types of weather are easier to act out than others. Rain, snow and hot sunshine are easy to portray symbolically, but fog, clouds, floods and black ice are harder. Encourage the children to challenge themselves and include storms with thunder and lightning, strong winds or rainbows.

The speeches and acts can be very dramatic and don't have to be realistic.

Invite the groups to perform to each other and to notice in which ways their acts are similar and in which ways they are different. If appropriate, announcers and actors could swap roles half way through their performances, or alternate the tasks.

Extensions/Variations
Talk about the types of weather experienced in other countries and places such as deserts, rainforests and the poles.

Invite one child at a time to take turns to make up a weather forecast to announce to the whole group and ask the other children to try to mime each weather type as they hear it.

Ask a practitioner to become the announcer and increase the pace, so that all children need to think and act more quickly to keep up with the changing weather.

Encourage children to take turns to mime a weather type or condition for the others to guess. Emphasize that good acting means they will be able to guess quickly – the aim is not to make it so difficult that nobody can tell what it is supposed to be!

Learning objectives/Early Learning Goals
* Develop and act out an experience or a narrative, working cooperatively within a group, and practise skills to perform it before others (EAD–BI; PSED–SCSA)
* Use language to imagine and recreate ideas and experiences for acting and role-play (CL–S)
* Speak confidently within a familiar group and take turns to perform a speech, asking for help if needed (PSED–SCSA)
* Speak clearly individually (CL–S; PSED–SCSA)
* Initiate discussion and conversation and attend to and take account of what others say, in order to plan and create a scenario or performance (PSED–MR)

Creating a storm

Themes
* Seasons/Weather/Elements
* Ourselves/Bodies/Families

Skills
* Acting/Mime
* Group work
* Craftwork

Equipment/Resources
A safe, clear floor space in which children can stand or move around together; craft materials and tools, fabric pieces, scarves or ribbons and torches; percussion instruments; books and pictures about storms for reference; music player; song: Umbrella (available to download from Brilliant Publications' website); CD player and CDs featuring children's action songs and popular and classical music on the theme of weather

Activity
Discuss weather and storms with the children and suggest that they try to re-create one. (Reassure any nervous children that it will only be a pretend storm and will not do any damage. Encourage them to overcome any fears through this role-play, but offer lots of support and allow them just to watch any parts they find too worrying.)

Provide art and craft equipment and materials, large pieces of fabric, scarves, ribbons and torches for children to create background scenes and props. Offer a selection of percussion instruments and support them in making their own shakers, drums and rhythm sticks.

Work with the whole group to plan, work out and perform their storm re-creation. For example, they might choose to twirl around with scarves and ribbons to symbolize winds, to use shakers and maracas as the sound of the rain beating down, to add drums and sticks played on walls and floor to symbolize hailstones, flashing torches as lightning and tambourines as thunder. Remind them that a storm builds gradually to a climax and then gradually dies down again to silence.

Extensions/Variations
Encourage children to use their bodies and voices to create the sounds they need (eg stamping, clapping, howling, blowing and saying 'pitter patter').

Find stories about characters (people and animals) caught out in a storm or other adverse weather conditions, such as snow or fog, and support children as they act them out.

Make a collection of action songs and rhymes on the theme of storms, rain and other weather conditions, including Umbrella. Play classical and popular music on the theme and invite children to make up dances and movements to fit the sounds and tunes.

Make up mime sequences involving putting on wet weather clothing, going out into the rain, using umbrellas, stamping in puddles, running home again, shaking umbrellas and hanging up all the clothes to dry, then sitting down indoors with a warming drink.

Learning objectives/Early Learning Goals
* Re-enact real, first-hand experiences through imaginative role play (EAD–BI)
* Create simple representations of events to develop a watchable movement sequence within the boundaries of a given storyline or narrative (EAD–BI)
* Operate simple technological equipment for use in dramatic activities (UW–T)
* Remember the aims of the activity and try various different strategies (PSED–MR, MFB)
* Use skills to explore concepts and ideas through representations (EAD–EUMM)
* Capture experiences and responses with a range of media (EAD–BI)

Capture the scene

Themes
* Stories/Fairy Tales
* Times of Year/Celebrations
* Ourselves/Bodies/Families

Skills
* Acting/Mime
* Confidence
* Craftwork

Equipment/Resources
A clear space in which adults and children can sit together comfortably as a group and move around safely and easily; craft materials for costumes and props; pens, scissors, glue sticks and sticky tape; digital cameras suitable for use by children and adults; computer and printer with photo paper

Activity
Explain to the group that you would like to take photographs of actors to make books and displays of stories, songs, rhymes, celebrations, special events, etc. Invite them to offer ideas.

Encourage children to mime characters, actions and events, making and using costume items and props as necessary and exaggerating expressions and freezing into positions to form recognizable scenes that can be photographed. Support them in taking pictures of each other, but ensure that enough are also taken by adults. For example, recreate Goldilocks and the Three Bears with one actor sitting up in a 'bed' and three actors standing around her and growling! Alternatively, make Humpty Dumpty with one actor lying on the ground and others galloping on horses and marching as soldiers all around him. Photograph a group of children blowing out candles on a play dough birthday cake, wearing Christmas hats and making paper chains, gathering around Diwali lamps or finding money in red envelopes for Chinese New Year.

Take photographs of all the scenes, print them out and support children in cutting them out and sticking them down in appropriate orders to make books, friezes, displays, etc.

Extensions/Variations
Invite small groups of children to recreate scenes of their choice that practitioners may photograph and print out. Gather the group and hold up the pictures one by one, inviting children to guess what they show. Discuss how effective expressions and exaggerated actions and positions make characters and scenes more obvious and easier to guess.

Encourage children to access cameras for themselves and take pictures of friends and activities whenever they choose to. Suggest that they might take pictures of art and craft or construction projects at various different stages, then make a display of the photographs to show how they made their pictures or models and what equipment and resources they used. Children who are reluctant to tidy up a detailed model or elaborate small world scenario can be encouraged to do so if they are able to keep photographs instead as a record of their work.

Learning objectives/Early Learning Goals
* Operate simple technological equipment for use in dramatic activities (UW–T)
* Portray characters and emotions through mime and expressive movement, understanding that the body can be used for communication (EAD–BI)
* Work cooperatively with others to act out a familiar part of a storyline (EAD–BI)
* Gain an awareness of the cultures and beliefs of others (UW–PC)
* Create simple representations of events, people and objects (EAD–BI)
* Use skills to explore concepts and ideas through representations (EAD–EUMM)
* Understand that different media can be combined to create new effects (EAD–EUMM)

Open the box

Themes
* Times of Year/Celebrations
* Ourselves/Bodies/Families

Skills
* Acting/Mime
* Singing
* Confidence
* Group work

Equipment/Resources
A safe, clear space in which children may move around and come together as a group; music player; instrumental track: If You've Happy and You Know it (available to download from Brilliant Publications' website)

Activity
Suggest to the children that they pretend that it is their birthday or Christmas, Diwali, Hanukkah, Chinese New Year, or any other time at which they might receive a present, such as a relative coming for a special visit or their family celebrating success or achievement.

Tell them that there is a huge pile of pretend boxes at the side of the room and that they may each choose one and inside will be something they would like to have.

Model miming the choosing of a box, lifting and carrying it to a space and sitting down to open it. Encourage all children and other practitioners to join in. Ask them to use movements and expressions to show whether their boxes are big or small, heavy or light, easy to carry or difficult to balance.

Ask everybody to open their pretend box slowly. Suggest that perhaps they need to untie or cut strings or ribbons, unpeel parcel tape or take out staples, before they can open the flaps and look inside. Demonstrate expressions of surprise and pleasure as you look inside your box and lift out the present, then invite the group to do the same.

Initiate a discussion about the pretend surprise presents, asking each person to describe what was inside their box. Praise interesting descriptions and original ideas. Mime can be fantasy and children may name anything, from sweets or a book to a dragon or a tractor!

Extensions/Variations
Instead of saying what was inside each box, ask children to mime their presents for the rest of the group to guess. They might eat some chocolate, draw with crayons, cuddle a teddy, play a trumpet, put on a new hat, bounce a ball or stroke a pet animal.

Play at pretending to climb inside the box to hide, then jumping out to surprise each other.

Sing an action song about a jack-in-a-box and practise squatting down to sleep silently, then waking and jumping up noisily in unison.

Demonstrate pleasure at the occasion and the gift by singing a song together, such as If You're Happy and You Know it.

Learning objectives/Early Learning Goals
* Portray characters and emotions through mime and expressive movement, understanding that the body can be used for communication (EAD–BI)
* Create simple representations of events, people, creatures or objects to develop a watchable movement sequence within the boundaries of a given storyline or narrative (EAD–BI)
* Memorize simple songs including words, tunes and appropriate actions, and sing them in unison with others, maintaining a steady speed and volume (EAD–EUMM)
* Think independently and offer ideas and opinions confidently to a group (PSED–SCSA; CL–S)
* Improve confidence and social skills through participation in a large group activity (PSED–MR, MFB; PD–MH)
* Follow instructions involving several ideas or actions (CL–U)

Join in for effect

Themes
* Stories/Fairy Tales
* Music/Sound

Skills
* Acting/Mime
* Listening
* Confidence

Equipment/Resources
A safe, clear space in which adults and children may sit comfortably in a group or a circle; a collection of percussion instruments; a version of the story: Jack and the Beanstalk; tape recorder and blank tape (or other recording device)

Activity
Read the story as a group and discuss the different sounds within it, such as the cow, the hen, the harp and the jingling bag of money, the different footsteps, the growing of the beanstalk, Jack climbing up, the giant stomping along, the chopping down of the beanstalk with an axe and the giant falling to earth with a crash.

Ask the children to suggest ways of creating sound effects with their voices and bodies. They could make mooing and clucking sounds, stamp their feet on the floor and clap their hands or tap them on the floor or on their knees.

Offer percussion instruments and decide how they could be used within the story. Bells could represent a money bag, maracas could indicate a beanstalk growing quietly during the night, tapping on a tambourine might make good footsteps for Jack, banging on a drum might sound like a stomping giant and cymbals could make a satisfying crash for the climax of the giant falling from the beanstalk as it is chopped down.

Narrate the story while the children create their sound effects to bring it to life. Record the story as you perform it together, then play it back for everybody to listen to.

Extensions/Variations
Challenge children to also create musical sound effects for the feelings and emotions contained within the story: Jack and his mother were sad when they had to sell their cow; the mother was angry when Jack gave her the beans and worried when he climbed up the beanstalk; the giant was fierce and terrifying; his wife was frightened for Jack's safety and made him hide; Jack was afraid when he climbed down quickly to get away from the giant and he and his mother were happy when the giant was gone and they had some money at last.

If children don't immediately agree on which instruments sound happy or sad, scary or angry, encourage them to try playing in different ways and at different volumes and speeds. Support them as they offer and discuss ideas, negotiate and compromise to reach agreement. Read or tell the story while they play the sounds that they have chosen. Use the same techniques to recreate new stories that you explore with the children, or any group favourites.

Learning objectives/Early Learning Goals
* Share ideas within a group and develop imagination around a theme, showing sensitivity to others' needs and feelings and forming positive relationships (PSED–MR)
* Explore the different sounds of instruments and use them appropriately to enhance performances (EAD–EUMM)
* Work, speak and listen appropriately as a member of a group, showing sensitivity to others' needs and feelings and responding with consideration (PSED–MR)
* Improve confidence and social skills through participation in a large group activity (PSED–MR, MFB; PD–MH)

Body language

Themes
* Ourselves/Bodies/Families
* Nursery Rhymes/Poems/Songs

Skills
* Singing
* Listening
* Group work
* Movement/Dance

Equipment/Resources
A clear, safe space to work in, without distractions. music player; songs: I've Got One Head, Toes and Knees, Click Your Fingers and Shaker Song; instrumental track: Head, Shoulders, Knees and Toes (songs and instrumental track available to download from Brilliant Publications' website)

Activity
Teach the song Head, Shoulders, Knees and Toes and encourage children to learn and join in with the words and appropriate actions.

Invite children to choose other parts of the body and support them in putting their ideas together in groups of four, then sing them as a group, pointing to the appropriate parts. For example: Elbow, Ankle, Chin and Fingers ...

Use this game as an opportunity to teach the names of many different body parts, by asking practitioners to offer suggestions alongside the children, such as wrists, heels, thighs and eyebrows. Support the children in fitting the new words into the tune, maintaining the rhythm.

Make a collection of action songs and rhymes featuring parts of the body, including I've Got One Head; Toes and Knees; Click Your Fingers and Shaker Song.

Extensions/Variations
Ask children, parents or practitioners who speak other languages to name body parts in these languages and try singing the song again, using as many different languages as possible.

Adapt other well-known songs in the same way, to suit particular themes or the children's interests. For example:

> Round and round the garden,
> with wings that fly so high,
> one flap, two flaps,
> fly up in the sky!

Invite children to take turns to perform songs for the group to watch, individually or with friends.

Learning objectives/Early Learning Goals
* Add to a growing repertoire of familiar songs and dances to be used in a variety of situations and activities (EAD–EUMM)
* Make up simple songs and rhythms and adapt familiar ones to fit particular themes (EAD–BI)
* Take cues to imitate, fill in or continue words and phrases in a song (CL–LA)
* Listen to songs and sing back what is heard, line by line, in order to learn them by heart, for immediate use or to add to a repertoire (EAD–EUMM)
* Follow instructions involving several ideas or actions (CL–U)
* Listen carefully and imitate and create movement in response to types of music (EAD–EUMM, BI)
* Memorize simple dances and confidently perform them to others, individually or within a group (EAD–EUMM; PSED–SCSA)

Atishoo, atishoo

Themes
* Ourselves/Bodies/Families
* Creatures/Animals/Birds/Plants

Skills
* Singing
* Movement/Dance
* Listening
* Confidence
* Group work

Equipment/Resources
A clear, safe space in which a group can work in a circle and in spaces

Activity
Teach the ring game Ring a Ring a Roses and encourage children to learn and join in with the words and the repeated movements (holding hands to walk in a circle, then letting go to 'fall' down).

Invite children to think of other movements and to take turns to suggest one, as you sing the song together. For example: 'Atishoo, atishoo, we all can – jump!' They may choose actions such as: wriggle, wobble, hop, spin, sway, hide, etc.

At first, allow any child to supply an action on cue, when they think of one. As they all become more confident, point to a different child each time to make it his turn to choose, encouraging the others to wait for their turns.

Everybody can copy the movement or action and then begin the song again.

Extensions/Variations
Practitioners can also take turns to choose actions and movements, introducing more specific or less well known ones, such as: Atishoo, atishoo, we jump three times! or Atishoo, atishoo, we skate and slide! or Atishoo, atishoo, push up towards the sky!

Increase the children's skills in balance, listening and concentration by including 'lack of movement', such as we stand on one leg or we all must freeze!

Invite children to think of creatures or plants to act out and sing: Atishoo, atishoo, we turn into dragons! or Atishoo, atishoo, we stand like a tree!

Ring a ring a roses...

Learning objectives/Early Learning Goals
* Memorize simple songs, including words, tunes and appropriate actions, and sing them in unison with others, maintaining a steady speed and volume (EAD–EUMM)
* Sing familiar songs with confidence and experiment with ways of changing them (EAD–EUMM)
* Communicate meaning and express feelings through movement, mime and dance (EAD–BI)
* Maintain attention, concentrate and move or stop quietly when appropriate (CL–LA)
* Initiate new combinations of movement and gesture to express and respond to ideas (EAD–BI)
* Match movements and actions to the space available (PD–MH)
* Develop good control and coordination in large and small movements (PD–MH)
* Attend to and take account of what others say in order to create a performance (PSED–MR)
* Think independently and offer ideas and opinions confidently to a group (PSED–SCSA; CL–S)
* Participate in a large group game or activity, understanding the need for rules and cooperation to ensure everybody's enjoyment (PSED–MR, MFB)

Counting down

Themes
* Colours/Shapes/Numbers
* Food/Drinks/Meals
* Creatures/Animals/Birds/Plants

Skills
* Singing
* Acting/Mime
* Confidence
* Craftwork

Equipment/Resources
A safe, clear space in which adults and children can sit together comfortably in a group; selected props to suit chosen songs: finger puppets, small toys, play money, toy food, etc; music player; instrumental track: Five Little Speckled Frogs (available to download from Brilliant Publications' website)

Activity
Choose finger rhymes and action songs that children are familiar with, such as: Five Currant Buns, Ten Fat Sausages, Three Little Monkeys, and Five Little Speckled Frogs. Use props to practise them as a group, making toys or puppets jump or hide on cue or lining up money or food items and taking them away.

Invite the children to pretend to be the objects or characters and talk about how to take cues and move at the appropriate times as the song is sung by the group. Split into small groups to perform songs, each supported by a practitioner. Set an example of sitting quietly to concentrate and listen carefully, with equal respect, to every performance.

Some songs just have parts for three or five children. Others can include a larger number, such as when five children each have a penny and buy one of the five currant buns or one child plays the part of the monkeys' mother and one is the doctor. Alternatively, an adult could play the extra parts. Most songs count down in ones, but some use twos, fives or tens.

Extensions/Variations
Encourage children to prepare rhymes or songs and actions within their small groups, to practise speaking or singing individually and to perform to each other in turn. Reassure them that mistakes don't matter, prompt and encourage them if necessary and emphasize that confidence and enthusiasm are the important elements of performing at this stage. Invite them to take a bow to indicate the end of their performance. Practitioners should clap each group as they bow and encourage the other children to join in.

Praise interesting ways of creating characters and events that children think of, such as funny voices, different walks or other movements and sound effects.

Support children in making masks, puppets or other props to enhance their performances.

Adapt the songs to suit any themes; being purple frogs, being dinosaurs jumping on the grass, pulling crackers with a pop and a bang or selling long carrots in a vegetable shop, etc.

Learning objectives/Early Learning Goals
* Confidently use songs and rhymes that involve number names, counting on and counting back in ones, twos, fives and tens, using fingers or whole body actions (M–N)
* Use intonation and different voices in action and character songs (CL–S)
* Memorize simple songs, including words, tunes and appropriate actions, and sing them individually, performing before others with confidence (EAD–EUMM; PSED–SCSA)
* Explore and develop skills of characterization within a small group, using different forms of language and intonation to imagine and recreate roles and experiences (CL–S)
* Thank an audience after a performance, through body language (EAD–BI)
* Work, speak and listen appropriately as a member of a group, showing sensitivity to others' needs and feelings and responding with consideration (PSED–MR)
* Use available resources to create costume pieces and props to support role-play (EAD–BI)

Make a noise

Themes
* Music/Sound
* Nursery Rhymes/Poems/Songs

Skills
* Singing
* Craftwork

Equipment/Resources
Recycled and found materials and containers, especially cylinders with lids, cardboard tubes, plastic pots and cartons and sturdy boxes; old pencils and pens, rulers and plastic spoons; craft materials and resources, such as stickers, ribbons, buttons, sequins, string and wool; coloured papers, pens, sticky tape and scissors; quantities of dried beans, lentils or rice

Activity
Offer children a wide range of equipment, materials and resources and work alongside them to make instruments such as shakers and drums, modelling ideas, skills and techniques and giving help and support to prevent frustration or when specifically requested by a child.

To make a simple shaker, choose a container and make sure one end is firmly closed, then add lentils or rice and make sure the other end is firmly closed. A lid must be attached with sticky tape, or a circle of paper could have slits cut around it and then be taped securely over the end of a cylinder or tube. Encourage children to decorate their shakers with pens and to attach craft pieces with sticky tape.

Any sturdy box or container can become a drum with some taping up and some decorations. Use broken pencils and worn out pens or cheap plastic rulers and spoons to make beaters for the drums, decorating them with wool or stickers.

Encourage children to wear aprons and to wash and dry their hands frequently and supervise them closely to ensure that they keep the rice and lentils away from their mouths.

Arrange singing times when children may play their instruments while they join in with familiar and favourite songs, or invite them to play them as they dance to recorded music.

Extensions/Variations
Help children to add string or wool to their instruments to make neck straps, so that they can wear them and use them while moving around as a marching band.

Try out different fillings for shakers, such as buttons, beads, paper fasteners or small bells, and experiment to find out which makes the loudest sound and which the softest sound. Ask children to compare the sounds of shakers with smaller and larger amounts of fillings in them (the contrast between the sounds made by a quantity of rice and by a few buttons is huge). Listen also to the different sounds made by pencils or spoons beating on various containers as drums.

Learning objectives/Early Learning Goals
* Sing familiar songs with confidence and experiment with ways of changing them, by selecting appropriate accompanying sounds and playing instruments to enhance performance (EAD–EUMM)
* Construct with a purpose in mind, using a variety of resources (EAD–EUMM)
* Confidently try new activities, choose resources independently and say when do or don't need help (PSED–SCSA)
* Work cooperatively, taking turns to use equipment and sharing resources (PSED–MR)
* Manage own basic personal and hygiene needs successfully (PD–HSC)

Play that tune

Themes
* Music/Sound
* Nursery Rhymes/Poems/Songs

Skills
* Singing
* Listening
* Group work

Equipment/Resources
A safe, clear floor space in which adults and children can sit comfortably in a circle; sets of two different percussion instruments; music player; instrumental tracks: Twinkle, Twinkle Little Star and/or Incy Wincy Spider (available to download from Brilliant Publications' website)

Activity
Choose a familiar song that has a repetitive tune and obvious pauses at the ends of lines, such as Baa Baa Black Sheep. Or try Twinkle, Twinkle Little Star or Incy Wincy Spider. Sing the song with the children, then give out instruments and sing it again, playing along with the rhythm and pausing at the obvious places.

Give each person two different percussion instruments that can easily be picked up and played quickly, such as maracas and bells. Sing the song together, playing one instrument for the first line, putting it down and picking up the other one to play the second line, then returning to the first instrument for the third line, and so on.

Take back the instruments and give out one instrument each, alternating the two around the circle. Sing the song and play the instruments again, but ask everybody to swap instruments at the end of each line by passing to the person on their right and receiving from the person on their left. (For health and safety reasons, avoid instruments played in the mouth when sharing them in this way.)

Extensions/Variations
Invite children to play lines of the song individually, taking turns in order around the circle. Sing the song as a group at first, while one child at a time plays their instrument. Eventually, children may feel confident enough to both sing and play lines individually, performing before the group.

If enough instruments are available, repeat the activity using three or four instruments in turn, or pass assorted different instruments around the circle, taking turns to play them all.

Ask children to suggest particularly suitable instruments for different song lyrics, such as maracas for rain, drums for marching or castanets for crocodiles.

Learning objectives/Early Learning Goals
* Memorize simple songs, including words, tunes and appropriate actions, and sing them both in unison and individually, maintaining a steady speed and volume and performing before others with confidence (EAD–EUMM; PSED–SCSA)
* Sing familiar songs with confidence and experiment with ways of changing them by selecting appropriate accompanying sounds and playing instruments to enhance performance (EAD–EUMM)
* Make up simple songs and rhythms and adapt familiar ones to fit particular themes (EAD—BI)
* Take cues to imitate, fill in or continue words or phrases in a song (CL–LA)
* Copy and tap out simple repeated rhythms and identify them as familiar names, words, phrases, rhymes or songs (EAD–EUMM)
* Explore the different sounds of instruments and use them appropriately to enhance performances (EAD–EUMM)
* Participate in a large group game or activity, understanding the need for rules and cooperation to ensure everybody's enjoyment (PSED–MR, MFB)

Walk or run

Themes
* Travelling/Places
* Nursery Rhymes/Poems/Songs

Skills
* Singing
* Movement/Dance
* Confidence

Equipment/Resources
A safe, clear floor space in which children can move around easily; music player; songs: Windows, Your Shoes, Shake 'n' Rattle and The Train (available to download from Brilliant Publications' website)

Activity
Choose a song that can be easily adapted for different movements and sing it with the children until they are familiar with the tune and the structure of the chorus. You could try: Let's Go Walking or She'll Be (Walking) Round the Mountain When She Comes or This Is the Way We Walk Around (to the tune of Here We Go Round the Mulberry Bush).

Ask children to suggest other travelling movements that use the whole body. Prompt or offer clues if necessary to ensure that they include many degrees of speed and different postures, such as: running, jogging, skipping, crawling, jumping, hopping and creeping.

Sing the song together as you move around, fitting words and movements together. Call out the next new movement at the end of each chorus, or invite children and other practitioners to take turns to do so. You may wish to end the activity by calling out a 'stopping' movement, such as: sit on the floor or go to sleep or freeze together.

Extensions/Variations
Ask children to 'catch the train' using symbolic circular arm movements, then to make up their own movements while following one behind another in a long line, rather than moving around each other in random spaces.

Fit four or five different movements together within one chorus of the song and perform them quickly, one after the other, as you sing.

Form small groups, each with one practitioner, and choose a set of movements independently of each other, then sing and perform them simultaneously while moving around each other. Praise children for concentrating on their own group, despite the distractions, for as long as possible and go on until they are laughing too much to continue.

Introduce other movement songs at appropriate times. Try Windows, Your Shoes, Shake 'n' Rattle and The Train.

Learning objectives/Early Learning Goals
* Sing familiar songs with confidence and experiment with ways of changing them (EAD–EUMM)
* Make up simple songs and rhythms and adapt familiar ones to fit particular themes (EAD–BI)
* Accurately anticipate and join in with repeated refrains and key phrases in songs, or respond with relevant actions (CL–LA)
* Move freely and with pleasure and confidence in a range of ways (PD–MH)
* Negotiate space successfully within a group, adjusting speed or changing direction to avoid obstacles or collisions (PD–MH)
* Think independently and offer ideas and opinions confidently to a group (PSED–SCSA; CL–S)
* Improve confidence and social skills through participation in a large group activity (PSED–MR, MFB; PD–MH)

Nimble fingers

Themes
* Nursery Rhymes/Poems/Songs
* Music/Sound
* Ourselves/Bodies/Families

Skills
* Singing
* Speech
* Listening
* Movement/Dance

Equipment/Resources
A safe, clear space in which adults and children can sit or stand together comfortably; music player; songs: I've Got One Head, Click Your Fingers and Shaker Song (available to download from Brilliant Publications' website); CD player and CDs featuring action and finger rhymes and songs

Activity
Ask the children: 'Did everybody bring their hands with them today?' If some take up the joke and say that they didn't, suggest that they find their spare ones in their pocket and put them on, or say that you will lend them some and pretend to throw some over to them.

Warm up hands and fingers by shutting them tightly as fists, opening and stretching them wide, hiding them behind your back, bringing them out suddenly, reaching up high in the air, pressing them down on the floor, shaking them loosely and wriggling fingers separately.

Invite everybody to participate as you sing and perform actions to a number of hand and finger rhymes and songs, including counting rhymes. Include well-known and less familiar ones in a random order, introduce new ones and end with one of the group's favourites. Encourage children to sing the words and perform the actions, maintaining a steady pace and rhythm. Try I've Got One Head, Click Your Fingers and Shaker Song.

Extensions/Variations
Prepare collections of rhymes and songs to fit particular themes and use them to extend children's understanding of, for example, parts of the body, creatures, weather or vehicles. Also use them to practise counting on and back using various numbers. Build up an extensive repertoire as a group and produce an appropriate song or rhyme for any situation. Invite children to sing and perform individually to the group whenever they would like to and offer appropriate support and encouragement.

Use finger rhymes and songs as a warm up or wind down activity at the beginning or end of any session and during spare minutes while the group is taking turns to do something, such as washing hands before lunch, putting on coats to go out or collecting paintings before going home. They can both calm and stimulate and bring the group together.

Make a CD player available to the children and demonstrate how to use it safely, so that they may choose to play songs and rhymes for independent role-play and just for listening.

Learning objectives/Early Learning Goals
* Memorize simple songs, including words, tunes and appropriate actions, and sing them in unison with others, maintaining a steady speed and volume, or individually, performing before others with confidence (EAD–EUMM; PSED–SCSA)
* Confidently use songs and rhymes that involve number names, counting on and counting back in ones, twos, fives and tens (M–N)
* Speak confidently within a familiar group and take turns to perform a speech, song or rhyme, asking for help if needed (PSED–SCSA)
* Listen to songs and sing back what is heard, line by line, in order to learn them by heart, for immediate use or to add to a repertoire (EAD–EUMM)
* Develop good control and coordination in large and small movements (PD–MH)

Rhyme time

Themes
* Nursery Rhymes/Poems/Songs
* Times of Year/Celebrations

Skills
* Singing
* Movement/Dance
* Acting/Mime
* Confidence
* Craftwork

Equipment/Resources
A safe, clear space in which children can move around each other easily; CD player; CDs featuring assorted nursery rhymes and popular children's songs; dressing-up outfits and props or materials to make them

Activity
Play the CD and act out each song in movement and mime, while singing along, as it plays. Encourage children to copy your actions and to create their own. For example: while Jack and Jill plays, walk 'up the hill', wind the bucket down into the well and up again, lift the heavy bucket of water, 'fall over', hold your head and then roll across the floor; while singing Humpty Dumpty, 'sit' in the air, 'fall' onto the floor, gallop like a horse, march like a soldier and then pretend to look at Humpty and shake your head. (It is vital that practitioners join in enthusiastically with every movement and action – rolling and wriggling on the floor as well as marching and stamping!)

Support children by calling out the name of each rhyme, or, as an extra challenge, leave them to guess from the opening bars or your first actions. Nursery rhymes are short and sung quickly, so performing lots in rapid succession, without knowing their order in advance, is both mentally and physically stimulating. Count each time with the children how many you achieved before everybody became exhausted!

Extensions/variations
Include a few new songs or rhymes, within a collection of familiar ones. Aim for some to involve human characters, some animals and some mini-beasts, plants, vehicles or weather.

Support the children in choosing their favourite rhymes and songs, practising them and preparing them for performance. Provide or make dressing up outfits, masks or props and encourage small groups of children to rehearse by performing to each other. Prepare an appropriate collection of short acts for a special occasion or end of term event and invite families into the setting to watch their children perform.

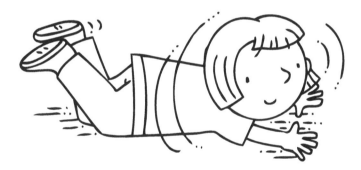

Learning objectives/Early Learning Goals
* Add to a growing repertoire of familiar songs and dances to be used in a variety of situations and activities (EAD–EUMM)
* Accurately anticipate and join in with repeated refrains and key phrases in songs, or respond with relevant actions (CL–LA)
* Explore and develop skills of characterization within a small group, by representing own ideas, thoughts and feelings through music, dance and role-play while acting out a familiar storyline within a song (EAD–BI)
* Listen carefully and imitate and create movement in response to types of music (EAD–EUMM, BI)
* Develop and act out an experience, a storyline or narrative, working cooperatively within a group, and practise skills to perform before others with confidence (EAD–BI; PSED–SCSA)
* Develop and use skills and explore concepts and ideas, embracing challenge and greater stimulation (EAD–BI)
* Use available resources to create costume pieces and props to support role play (EAD–BI)

Pleased to meet you

Themes
* Ourselves/Bodies/Families
* Colours/Shapes/Numbers

Skills
* Speech
* Listening
* Confidence
* Group work

Equipment/Resources
A clear, safe space in which adults and children can sit comfortably in a circle; music player; song: 'Hello' – Bounce (available to download from Brilliant Publications' website)

Activity
Gather the group of practitioners and children together and invite them to sit in a circle. Turn to the child on your right and offer your hand, saying: 'Hello, my name is (Debbie).'

Encourage the child to shake your hand and reply: 'Hello, my name is (Andy).' Nod with interest, repeat the child's name clearly and praise him for responding. Suggest that the child repeats the activity with the person on his right and that, in this way, introductions are made around the circle until the child to the left of the leader introduces himself.

Encourage everybody to listen as each person speaks and to remember names they didn't know. Invite children to say hello in their first languages; they need not all speak in English.

Extensions/Variations
Encourage pairs of children to introduce themselves to each other, shaking hands confidently and taking turns to speak and to reply.

If the children are of different nationalities, suggest that they both learn to say hello in both languages. For example: 'Hola, me llamo Maria.' 'Hola Maria. Hello, my name is Tess.' 'Hello Tess.'

If a child speaks without shaking hands, try to gently take his hand and then release it, but don't insist if he prefers not to accept the contact. If he shakes hands but remains silent, gently prompt him with, 'And your name is ...?' If a child doesn't reply, other children may tell you his name. Make eye contact, say his name with a smile and then move on.

Confident children could extend their conversations by naming their favourite colours or shapes or stating how many siblings they have, etc.

Offer this activity regularly, encouraging children to sit in different places around the circle and not always next to their chosen friends, so that they have opportunities to speak directly to different members of the group. Children who do not participate at first will suddenly achieve the confidence or the understanding to enjoy this activity, if they are not made to feel under pressure to 'perform' in front of the group before they are ready.

Introduce the children to the song 'Hello'– Bounce and then invite them to use it when introducing themselves to each other.

Learning objectives/Early Learning Goals
* Speak confidently within a familiar group, taking turns to initiate discussion and speech (PSED–SCSA)
* Speak clearly individually (CL–S; PSED–SCSA)
* Attend to and take account of what others say (PSED–MR)
* Have an awareness of and an interest in cultural and language differences (UW–PC)
* Improve confidence and social skills through participation in a large group activity (PSED–MR, MFB, PD–MH)
* Follow instructions involving several ideas or actions (CL–U)

Do you hear what I say?

Themes
* Ourselves/Bodies/Families
* Nursery Rhymes/Poems/Songs

Skills
* Speech
* Listening
* Confidence
* Group work

Equipment/Resources
A long enough room, hall or corridor with a safe space for a group of children to stand at each end; microphone plugged into an amplifier and speaker, or without a wire (a radio microphone), or a toy 'echo microphone'

Activity
Invite the children to move into two groups, each with one or more practitioners, and to stand and face each other from the two ends of the room, hall or corridor.

Ask one group to shout loudly to the other. Suggest something simple like: 'Good morning!' or 'We can see you!' Ask the second group to shout a similar reply. Move on to something a little more complicated, such as: 'We are the children of (name of setting)!'

Explain that it is hard to hear people when they shout and demonstrate how to speak extra clearly (in an exaggerated way) and how to raise the voice only slightly and push it towards the other group.

Give these skills their correct names – enunciation and projection.

Ask the groups to try again, using these techniques, and they should discover that they can understand each other much more easily.

Demonstrate the use of a microphone, speaking into it clearly and explaining that you don't need to speak as loudly or work so hard to project the voice, but enunciation is still very important.

Offer children the opportunity to try using the microphone in turn. Support them as they learn to hold it at the right distance, close to but not touching their mouths.

Extensions/Variations
Encourage the groups to discover for themselves the benefits of speaking in unison – starting together after '1, 2, 3' – rather than at random times, by trying one and then the other, in the same way.

Suggest that the two groups take cues from each other and speak rhymes together. For example: Group A says, Twinkle, twinkle, little star and Group B says, How I wonder what you are, then Group A continues with Up above the world so high, and so on.

Learning objectives/Early Learning Goals
* Improve enunciation in order to express words, ideas and messages clearly, showing awareness of listeners' needs (CL–S)
* Take cues confidently to fill in the missing word or phrase in a known rhyme, story or song (L--R)
* Improve voice projection (CL–S; PSED–SCSA)
* Speak clearly in unison (CL–S; PSED–SCSA)
* Notice changes in what is heard (CL–LA)
* Improve confidence and social skills through participation in a large group activity (PSED–MR, MFB, PD–MH)
* Select and use technology for particular purposes (UW–T)
* Understand the need for rules and cooperation to ensure everybody's enjoyment (PSED–MR, MFB)

Food on the move

Themes
* Food/Drinks/Meals
* Times of Year/Celebrations

Skills
* Speech
* Acting/Mime
* Movement/Dance
* Singing

Equipment/Resources
A clear space in which adults and children can move around safely and easily; music player; instrumental track: Polly Put the Kettle On (available to download from Brilliant Publications' website)

Activity
Ask children to think of foods and drinks that move in different ways. Encourage them to offer ideas and to volunteer to explain or demonstrate further if they feel confident to do so. Develop mimes and actions together to illustrate various meals.

Examples of good foods and drinks to mime might be: wobbly jellies, popping corn, tossing pancakes, fizzy drinks, slippery spaghetti, sizzling bacon and bendy bananas and cucumbers.

Play games involving children acting out foods as a practitioner calls them out, or individuals or groups miming foods for everybody else to guess, or creating a shopping list together and trying to remember and pretend to be the foods and drinks in the agreed order.

Extensions/Variations
Talk about particular foods for special places, occasions or events and invite children to mime or act out short scenes, individually or as small groups, such as eating popcorn and drinking through straws while watching a film at the cinema, toasting the bride and groom with champagne at a wedding, or flipping pancakes for Shrove Tuesday.

Sing a song about preparing food or drinks, such as Polly Put the Kettle On, and prepare an acted sequence to perform as you sing.

Sing other appropriate songs about foods and drinks, such as Ten Fat Sausages, Sweet Gingerbread Man, Hot Cross Buns and One Potato, Two Potato, and add actions and sound effects. You could change the lyrics of any popular song to include a favourite food that doesn't usually feature in children's songs and rhymes.

Learning objectives/Early Learning Goals
* Speak confidently within a familiar group and take turns to initiate discussion, describe an activity or perform a speech, song or rhyme, asking for help if needed (PSED–SCSA)
* Create simple representations of events, people, creatures or objects to develop a watchable movement sequence within the boundaries of a given storyline or narrative (EAD–BI)
* Re-enact real, first-hand experiences through imaginative role-play (EAD–BI)
* Work cooperatively with others to act out a familiar part of a storyline (EAD–BI)
* Communicate meaning and express feelings through movement, mime and dance in various styles (EAD–BI)
* Add to a growing repertoire of familiar songs and dances to be used in a variety of situations and activities (EAD–EUMM)
* Make up simple songs and rhythms and adapt familiar ones to fit particular themes (EAD–BI)

Let's build a house

Themes
* Building/Homes
* Seasons/Weather/Elements
* People Who Help Us/Occupations

Skills
* Speech
* Movement/Dance
* Acting/Mime
* Group work

Equipment/Resources
A safe, clear space in which children may move around easily; a collection of pictures of different types of houses, from books, posters and the Internet

Activity
Initiate a discussion about houses and look at pictures with the children, talking about similarities and differences, the materials that houses can be made from and the tools and machines that are used to build them. Invite children to join you in building a pretend house. Make suggestions and model movements, such as laying bricks for the walls, sawing wood for the windows and using a hammer and nails to put the window frames into place. Encourage all ideas and support children in developing mimes and using pretend props.

Ask children to describe their pretend houses and to decide whether they are making a big house or a small one, a tall, thin one, a long, low one or an unusually shaped one. They may choose to act out carrying heavy bricks or pushing them in a barrow, driving a truck or lifting heavy frames with a crane. Some of the children may be knowledgeable about

tools used in the home, such as drills, sanders and screwdrivers. Many of them will make noises to represent machinery and tools as they use them. Praise especially imaginative or realistic acts, encouraging children to share ideas and to take notice of what others are doing.

Talk about health and safety and the need to wear protective clothing, helmets, boots, pads and ear protectors when working on a building site or using noisy machinery.

Sit inside your pretend houses and talk about how well they protect you from the cold, heat, rain, snow, wind and storms. Alternatively, pretend that there is a hole in the roof and begin a new game to repair it quickly before a storm comes!

Extensions/Variations
Provide large bricks, play tools, dressing up outfits and helmets and other appropriate equipment to create a building site role-play area, preferably outside or both outdoors and indoors. Include sand and mud as building materials. Agree on some safety rules with the children, such as being aware of each other, using tools carefully, not stacking bricks too high and not putting anything into their mouths.

Encourage children to work together in groups to build pretend houses, talking about teamwork on a building site and people's different jobs and skills. Work alongside children to build homes for small world people, using a variety of different construction kits

Learning objectives/Early Learning Goals
* Use language to imagine and recreate ideas and experiences for acting and role-play (CL–S)
* Use talk to organize, sequence and clarify thinking, ideas, feelings and events when planning scenarios or performances (CL–S)
* Develop good control and coordination in large and small movements (PD–MH)
* Match movements and actions to the space available (PD–MH)
* Share ideas within a group and develop imagination around a theme, showing sensitivity to others' needs and feelings and forming positive relationships (PSED–MR)
* Follow simple safety rules, tackle new challenges and manage appropriate risks (PD–MH, HSC; PSED–SCSA)

What's happening in the garden?

Themes
* Seasons/Weather/Elements
* Travelling/Places

Skills
* Speech
* Confidence
* Movement/Dance
* Acting/Mime

Equipment/Resources
A clear space to work in with a safe, clean floor or ground surface; music player; songs: Windows, The Train and Aeroplane (available to download from Brilliant Publications' website)

Activity
Invite the children to come into your pretend garden. Encourage them to act and pretend by copying your movements and actions, as you use your voice and body enthusiastically. For example, say: 'Let's hide behind the trees – and now, let's – jump out! Let's rake up all the leaves into a pile. Shall we jump into them? Oh dear, we've made the leaves fly away! We need to rake them up again. Come on, we'll put them into the wheelbarrow and wheel them down to the compost heap. Now we can tip them all out. Let's get a spade and a watering can from the shed and some seeds to plant. Dig a hole first, put the seeds in and cover them up. Now take the watering can to the tap and fill it up. It's splashy! It's so heavy to carry when it's full of water! Sprinkle a little water over the seeds ...' and so on. Describe what you are doing as you make each movement.

As soon as the children understand the game, they will begin to offer ideas of their own, that you can integrate into the action. Try to use all ideas and allow the scenario to go wherever the children's imaginations take it. When it reaches its natural end, praise the children as a group: 'What a good story you made together!'

Extensions/Variations
Start mimes and acted stories and sequences from other points, such as: going to the playground with a ball, lifting and stacking heavy boxes into a wobbly tower, making a birthday cake, a tray of buns or pancakes, catching a train, bus or aeroplane and going on a journey, rowing a boat, falling into the river or sea and swimming to an island.

Encourage children to create mimed sequences to accompany songs such as Windows, The Train and Aeroplane.

Learning objectives/Early Learning Goals
* Use language to imagine and recreate ideas and experiences for acting and role-play (CL–S)
* Initiate new combinations of movement and gesture to express and respond to feelings/ideas (EAD–BI)
* Develop good control and coordination in large and small movements (PD–MH)
* Think independently and offer ideas and opinions confidently to a group (PSED–SCSA; CL–S)
* Re-enact real, first-hand experiences through imaginative role-play (EAD–BI)
* Create simple representations of events, people, creatures or objects to develop a watchable movement sequence within the boundaries of a given storyline or narrative (EAD–BI)
* Share ideas within a group and develop imagination around a theme, showing sensitivity to others' needs and feelings and forming positive relationships (PSED–MR)

Answer me

Themes
* Stories/Fairy Tales
* Creatures/Animals/Birds/Plants
* Building/Homes

Skills
* Speech
* Listening

Equipment/Resources
A safe, clear space in which adults and children may stand in three lines, close to each other; a version of The Three Little Pigs story

Activity
Read the story The Three Little Pigs with the children.

Invite children to stand in three lines, preferably with one or more practitioners in each line, forming a triangle shape and all facing in towards the centre. Ask the first line to pretend to be wolves and say, 'Little pig, little pig, let me come in.' Ask the second line to pretend to be pigs and reply, 'No, no, by the hair on my chinny chin chin, I will not let you in!' Then ask the third line to pretend to be wolves and say, 'Then I'll huff and I'll puff and I'll blow your house in!'

Encourage all the children to try out different voices to sound like wolves and little pigs.

Repeat the activity several times, beginning with a different line each time, so that everybody can have a turn at playing each role and making each speech. Stop prompting as soon as possible, so that children learn to take cues from each other and come in correctly.

Extensions/Variations
Initiate a discussion of the story with the children and ask for suggestions of other speeches that the little pigs and the wolf made and put them together in threes for the three lines to deliver to each other in the same way. For example: 'I built a house of straw'; 'I built a house of sticks'; 'I built a house of bricks'.

A shorter one, to increase the challenge of cue-taking and character voices, might be: 'I'll huff!'; 'And I'll puff!'; 'And I'll blow your house down!' (Blowing sounds could be added!)

Learning objectives/Early Learning Goals
* Speak clearly in unison (CL–S; PSED–SCSA)
* Improve enunciation, in order to express words, ideas and messages clearly, showing awareness of listeners' needs (CL–S)
* Take cues confidently to speak in character to continue a storyline or narrative (L–R)
* Experiment with words and sounds, rhythm, intonation, character voices and speeches, sound effects and differences in speed and volume in songs, rhymes and stories (CL–S; L–R)
* Listen to stories, songs or rhymes with increasing attention and recall, in order to discuss and recreate all or parts of them (CL–LA)
* Initiate discussion and conversation and attend to and take account of what others say, in order to plan and create a scenario or performance (PSED–MR)

Speak in character

Themes
* Stories/Fairy Tales
* People Who Help Us/Occupations

Skills
* Speech
* Singing
* Confidence
* Craftwork

Equipment/Resources
A safe, clear space in which adults and children can sit together comfortably in a group; popular stories or fairy tales that involve speeches and dialogues

Activity
Read stories to the group and talk about what the characters say to each other. Begin with well-known dramatic speeches, such as the ones between the wolf and the little pigs, the troll and the Billy Goats Gruff or the wolf and Red Riding Hood. Ask another practitioner to perform the dialogue with you as an example for the children.

Invite children to perform speeches in turn, working in pairs or small groups. Emphasize to them that the aim is to speak with confidence and expression, rather than to worry about getting particular words right. If they think about characters and a storyline that they know well, they will be able to create a dialogue of their own that others will recognize and understand. Encourage children to speak slowly, calmly and loudly enough to enunciate clearly and project their voices in performance.

As children become more confident, suggest that they continue stories through dialogue, deciding what the characters would have said and done next, after the events in the story.

Extensions/Variations
Encourage children to dress up, make props and use furniture and other items as set, in order to perform their dialogues as scenes for others to watch. Invite them to explain their costumes, set and props, but remind them that their speeches are still the most important parts of the scenes and that they should not rely on miming with props to tell their stories.

Suggest that children could develop their characters and speeches further by using different voices or developing expressive voices to display excitement, fear or anger.

Allow children to include songs or rhymes as well as speeches for their scenes and characters and to sing or speak in unison as well as individually.

Learning objectives/Early Learning Goals
* Use language to imagine and recreate ideas and experiences for acting and role-play (CL–S)
* Speak confidently within a familiar group and take turns to perform a speech, song or rhyme, asking for help if needed (PSED–SCSA)
* Improve enunciation, in order to express words, ideas and messages clearly, showing awareness of listeners' needs (CL–S)
* Speak clearly individually and improve voice projection (CL–S; PSED–SCSA)
* Experiment with words and sounds, rhythm, intonation, character voices and speeches, sound effects and differences in speed and volume in songs, rhymes and stories (CL–S; L–R)
* Talk about and explain the symbolic use of furniture and objects as props (CL–S)
* Use intonation and different voices in action and character songs (CL–S)
* Explore and develop skills of characterization within a small group, by representing own ideas, thoughts and feelings through music, dance and role play while acting out a familiar storyline within a song (EAD–BI)
* Lead a group confidently (PSED–SCSA, MR)
* Use available resources to create costume pieces and props to support role-play (EAD–BI)

Story posters

Themes

* Stories/Fairy Tales
* Colours/Shapes/Numbers

Skills

* Speech
* Listening
* Confidence
* Group work
* Craftwork

Equipment/Resources

Selection of papers, pens, pencils, crayons, scissors and glue sticks; wide variety of books containing popular children's stories

Activity

Invite small groups of children to choose a favourite story that they would like to re-create and perform (a different story for each group). Allocate a specific supporting adult to each group. Make a selection of books and other resources available and suggest that they work together to find versions of their chosen stories.

Offer them a free choice of drawing and writing materials and ask them to make posters advertising their forthcoming performances. Each group may choose to collaborate and make one larger poster, or to make smaller posters as pairs or individuals.

Encourage children to look through books for ideas on how to draw characters and scenes from their

stories and to read names and key words to remind them of the plots.

Support them as they decide which information should be included on a poster (title, date, time, actors, etc.) and to write the words they need. Remind them that they can copy the spellings of the story titles and find simple words in books. They may be able to write their own names independently.

Extensions/Variations

Support children in using a computer program to create posters that combine words, numbers, pictures, colours and shapes in various formats and printing them out.

Invite children to write and illustrate their own versions of the stories as zigzag books.

Take photographs of the children acting out their stories and invite them to use the pictures and their own words to make a display, an album or a storybook.

Encourage children to use popular characters and settings or traditional tales as starting points and to make up their own stories or alternative endings to act out.

Learning objectives/Early Learning Goals

* Use talk to organize, sequence and clarify thinking, ideas, feelings and events when planning scenarios or performances (CL–S)
* Explain own knowledge and understanding, ask appropriate questions of others, take account of others' ideas and resolve conflicts through compromise (PSED–MR)
* Listen to stories, songs or rhymes with increasing attention and recall, in order to discuss and recreate all or parts of them (CL–LA)
* Recognize, rhythm, rhyme and alliteration and use them in activities (L–R)
* Think independently and offer ideas and opinions confidently to a group (PSED–SCSA; CL–S)
* Follow instructions involving several ideas or actions (CL–U)
* Use identifiable letters and phonic knowledge to communicate meaning (L–W)
* Handle equipment and tools effectively, including pencils for drawing and writing (PD–MH)
* Represent own ideas, thoughts and feelings through art and design (EAD–BI)
* Use a simple program on a computer to produce text, pictures and designs (UW–T)

Square rhymes

Themes
* Nursery Rhymes/Poems/Songs
* Food/Drinks/Meals

Skills
* Speech
* Listening
* Confidence

Equipment/Resources
A safe, clear space in which adults and children can stand together comfortably in lines and groups

Activity
Choose a favourite rhyme that the children know well and practise speaking (not singing) it together as a group. Support the children as they divide themselves into four groups. Make sure that there is an equal number of children and a practitioner in each group if possible. Invite the groups to form lines and to stand facing inwards as the four sides of a square. Call the lines A B C and D and leave small gaps at the corners of the square, so that each child knows which line he belongs to.

Divide the rhyme into four lines and ask the groups to speak one line of the rhyme each in turn, taking their cue from each other and joining in without a pause. Humpty Dumpty works well. Begin with the order ABCD, then repeat the activity with the lines speaking in different orders, such as: DCBA, BDAC and CADB. Some food rhymes, such as Ten Fat Sausages and Jelly On A Plate, are simple to divide and chant and appealing to the children. Or build up the challenge gradually, using Hot Cross Buns. First divide the rhyme into four longer lines and speak one line each (ABCD). Then divide it into eight shorter lines and speak two lines each (ABCDABCD).

Encourage clear enunciation and voice projection into the centre of the square, so that everybody can hear and understand the rhymes and perform their parts with confidence.

Extensions/Variations
Try a longer rhyme, such as Baa Baa Black Sheep or Incy Wincy Spider, using eight lines and asking each group to speak twice in turn, taking cues from lines that are not standing next to them. For example: ACBDACBD.

Whisper a different rhyme to each group in turn and ask them to speak the first line. Encourage the other groups to immediately take their cues and continue the rhyme around the square without preparation.

Invite each group to secretly choose a rhyme together and to work on saying a line or section each, then to perform it to the other groups. Encourage them to add interest by using a variety of speeds, volumes and rhythms and different character voices.

Learning objectives/Early Learning Goals
* Speak clearly, both in unison and individually (CL–S; PSED–SCSA)
* Improve voice projection (CL–S; PSED–SCSA)
* Take cues confidently to fill in the missing word or phrase in a well-known rhyme, or to speak in character to continue a narrative (L–R)
* Improve enunciation, in order to express words, ideas and messages clearly, showing awareness of listeners' needs (CL–S)
* Experiment with words and sounds, rhythm, intonation, character voices and speeches, sound effects and differences in speed and volume in songs, rhymes and stories (CL–S; L–R)
* Listen to stories, songs or rhymes with increasing attention and recall, in order to discuss and recreate all or parts of them (CL–LA)
* Recognize rhythm, rhyme and alliteration and use them in activities (L–R)
* Initiate discussion and conversation and attend to and take account of what others say, in order to plan and create a scenario or performance (PSED–MR)
* Improve confidence and social skills through participation in a large group activity (PSED–MR, MFB; PD–MH)

Make an echo

Themes
* Colours/Shapes/Numbers
* Nursery Rhymes/Poems/Songs

Skills
* Listening
* Confidence
* Group work

Equipment/Resources
A safe, clear, quiet space in which adults and children can sit or stand and listen, without distractions; percussion instruments which can be tapped, beaten or banged with hands or beaters, such as drums, tambourines and triangles

Activity
Invite the children to form two groups, each with one or more practitioners (preferably two or three, depending on the size of the group) and to sit or stand facing each other.

Ask everybody to clap three times, then four times, then once loudly and twice softly, etc. Continue to give simple instructions like this until all children are focused, listening and responding and trying to follow them correctly.

Join one group and clap some beats in a simple rhythm. Ask the practitioners in the other group to copy the rhythm, recreating the sound exactly, like an echo. Repeat this several times with different rhythms and ask the children of the second group to join in.

Ask a practitioner of the second group to clap some beats in a rhythm for the first group to echo in the same way.

Offer this activity frequently and gradually increase the complexity of the rhythms and the number of beats, as the groups continue to take turns to create and to echo them. Start with three or four beats in a rhythm and (over several sessions) work up to ten.

Extensions/Variations
Try clapping the rhythms of the first lines of nursery rhymes and popular songs and asking the other group to guess which ones they are as they copy them.

Ask everybody with a one syllable name to clap once, those with two syllables to clap twice, those with three to clap three times and any with four or more to clap their syllables.

Stamp feet, tap knees or bang on the floor, instead of clapping, to vary any of the activities. Use percussion instruments to create rhythms in the same way.

Use a selection of differently coloured instruments and ask, for example, those with red tambourines or white castanets to make a rhythm for those with blue tambourines or brown castanets to copy.

Stand in different formations, beginning with a circle and moving on to a square and a triangle. Ask one practitioner or child to create a simple rhythm and each person to copy it in turn to move around the shape and back to the starting point.

Learning objectives/Early Learning Goals
* Copy and tap out simple repeated rhythms and identify them as familiar names, words, phrases, rhymes or songs (EAD–EUMM)
* Count beats and reproduce specific numbers of beats as necessary (M–N)
* Lead a group confidently (PSED–SCSA, MR)
* Improve confidence and social skills through participation in a large group activity (PSED–MR, MFB; PD–MH)
* Remember rules and aims of the game or activity and try various different strategies (PSED–MR, MFB)

Balancing act

Themes
* Colours/Shapes/Numbers
* Ourselves/Bodies/Families
* Creatures/Animals/Birds/Plants

Skills
* Listening
* Group work
* Movement/Dance
* Confidence

Equipment/Resources
A clear space to work in with a safe, clean floor or ground surface; percussion instruments such as drums or tambourines; music player; song: Shake 'n' Rattle (available to download from Brilliant Publications' website)

Activity
Invite children to sit together in a group or a circle and provide them with drums, tambourines or any instruments that can be tapped with hands or beaters. Encourage them to recite numbers in order and tap a beat for each one, maintaining a steady rhythm of one beat per second.

Ask half of the group to continue to count seconds through making beats, while the others practise some balancing skills. Find out how many seconds they can balance for, first on two hands and one foot, then one hand and one foot, then standing on one leg only. Swap the groups over, so that each child has a turn to play beats and a turn to balance.

Repeat the activity, but this time ask children to combine two or three different balances while counting the beats, such as: balance on two hands and one foot for eleven seconds, then on one hand and one foot for seven seconds, then on one foot only for five seconds.

End the activity by playing the song Shake 'n' Rattle and performing the actions, freezing and balancing for as long as possible on 'stop' at the end.

Extensions/Variations
Give the different balances colour names instead of descriptions, such as pink for standing on one leg (because flamingoes do that) and brown for one hand and one foot (because monkeys swing from trees like that). Call out only the colours and ask children to try to remember what to do for each one.

Try other balances, such as sitting on the floor with both hands and feet in the air, or lifting up the feet while kneeling.

Ask children to create shapes through bending, leaning and balancing, alone or with others, and to hold the shapes for a certain number of seconds.

Learning objectives/Early Learning Goals
* Count beats and reproduce specific numbers of beats as necessary (M–N)
* Follow instructions involving several ideas or actions (CL–U)
* Count aloud reliably using numbers 1–10 or 1–20 in order while playing a group game, to make a number of steps or jumps or to wait for a number of seconds (M–N)
* Develop good control in large and small movements (PD–MH)
* Learn and use vocabulary of movement and controlled effort (PD–MH)
* Improve confidence and social skills through participation in a large group activity (PSED–MR, MFB; PD–MH)
* Develop and use skills and explore concepts and ideas, embracing challenge and greater stimulation (EAD–BI)

Sailing into the wind

Themes
* Colours/Shapes/Numbers
* Seasons/Weather/Elements
* Travelling/Places

Skills
* Listening
* Group work
* Confidence
* Acting/Mime

Equipment/Resources
A clear space to work in with a safe, clean floor or ground surface; large pieces of fabric in different colours, cut into different shapes such as triangles, circles, squares, rectangles and diamonds

Activity
Give each child a large fabric shape. (If you don't have lots of different fabrics, work with a small group at a time.) Ask the children to sit in spaces and to hold up their fabric shapes, as though they are in boats with sails.

Tell a simple story or narrative and ask the children to respond to the different types of weather that you mention through mime. While the air is calm and warm, they can sail along, then make the sails ripple slightly as a breeze begins and flap more strongly as the wind blows harder, rock the boat as the waves rise higher, hide from the storm, fall into the water as the boat capsizes, swim back and climb in to hold up the sail again, then give up and put it down as the wind drops completely and row the boat home.

Make the narrative more complicated by saying, for example, that the boats with red sails sailed through the strong winds and the boats with yellow sails were hit by a storm, but the boats with blue sails had no wind and had to row. Alternatively, ask the children to listen carefully for their shapes and say that the triangular sails drifted in a gentle breeze, but the square sails flapped hard in a storm.

Introduce numbers too by asking the boats to row for twenty seconds until the wind starts to blow again and then sail for fifteen seconds until they stop at the shore.

Extensions/Variations
Scatter coloured hoops across the floor. Call out how many rowers should sit in each coloured boat, such as five in each blue boat and six in each red boat, and ask children to organize themselves to sit there. Then call out different numbers and ask them all to move around.

Attach the fabric sails to sticks or tubes and use them as flags. Play a game asking the children to wave the flags as you call out the shapes. For example, call for all the circles to wave up and down, the triangles to wave quickly from side from side, the rectangles to wave slowly from side to side and the squares to wave around and around.

Learning objectives/Early Learning Goals
* Listen to stories, songs or rhymes with increasing attention and recall, in order to discuss and recreate all or parts of them (CL–LA)
* Follow instructions involving several ideas or actions (CL–U)
* Count aloud reliably using numbers 1–10 or 1–20 in order while playing a group game, to make a number of steps or jumps or to wait for a number of seconds (M–N)
* Improve confidence and social skills through participation in a large group activity (PSED–MR, MFB; PD–MH)
* Create simple representations of events, people, creatures or objects to develop a watchable movement sequence within the boundaries of a given storyline or narrative (EAD–BI)

Loud or soft?

Themes
* Music/Sound
* Nursery Rhymes/Poems/Songs

Skills
* Listening
* Confidence

Equipment/Resources
A safe, clear space in which adults and children may sit comfortably in a group or a circle; a collection of percussion instruments; music player; instrumental track: Incy Wincy Spider (available to download from Brilliant Publications' website)

Activity
Ask children to think of sounds that are loud or noisy, such as: thunder, aeroplanes, motorbikes, fireworks, shouting and lions roaring. Then ask them to think of sounds that are soft or quiet, such as: gently falling rain, a breeze in the trees, scissors cutting paper, whispering and cats purring. Offer assorted percussion instruments and ask children to say which they think make louder sounds and which softer sounds.

Challenge them to try playing each one loudly and then softly. They will probably find that, although some are better for loud or soft sounds, most of them can be played in either way and may sound quite different.

Choose two instruments that you will hold up as signals, one to represent playing loudly, such as a drum) and one to represent playing softly (such as a maraca). Hold up the drum and encourage the children to play their instruments very loudly. Hold up the maraca and encourage them to play very softly. Play a group game in which you hold up the instruments in turn, swapping them more and more frequently and occasionally holding up the same one for a few consecutive times, to try to 'catch them out'.

Extensions/Variations
Play the game without instruments, inviting children to clap their hands, stamp their feet, tap on their knees or bang on the floor to make sounds instead.

Ask the children to clap their hands or play an instrument as quickly as they can and then as slowly as they can. Children often think that quickly means loudly and slowly means softly, so work on making sounds that are loud and quick and sounds that are loud and slow, sounds that are soft and quick and sounds that are soft and slow. Try playing loud and slow beats as you sing Humpty Dumpty and soft and quick beats for Incy Wincy Spider.

Offer further challenge by asking who can make four slow beats or five quick beats, or even two slow beats, followed by three quick beats, followed by two slow beats again. Develop this idea with some children to allow them to tap out simple repeated rhythms to accompany popular simple songs. For example: clap, tap on the floor or beat with a drumstick while you sing Peter Works with One Hammer, using four quick beats, nine slower beats, four quick beats, six slower beats.

Learning objectives/Early Learning Goals
* Explore the different sounds of instruments and use them appropriately to enhance performances (EAD–EUMM)
* Notice changes in what is heard (CL–LA)
* Count beats and reproduce specific numbers of beats as necessary (M–N)
* Copy and tap out simple repeated rhythms and identify them as familiar names, words, phrases, rhymes and songs (EAD–EUMM)
* Understand a new concept and verbalize thinking and understanding (CL–U, S)
* Develop and use skills and explore concepts and ideas, embracing challenge and greater stimulation (EAD–BI)
* Improve confidence and social skills through participation in a large group activity (PSED–MR, MFB; PD–MH)

Movement match

Themes
* Travelling/Places
* Music/Sound

Skills
* Listening
* Movement/Dance
* Acting/Mime
* Craftwork
* Confidence

Equipment/Resources
A safe, clear floor space in which children can move around easily; three percussion instruments that make very different sounds; coloured paper and card, crêpe and tissue papers, staplers and sticky tape

Activity
Play a soft and tinkling instrument, such as bells or a triangle, and invite children to tiptoe around softly and gently in time to the sound. Maintain a simple rhythm as you shake or tap the instrument, such as four beats and a rest or two quick beats then two slow beats. Then play a louder instrument, such as wood blocks or a tambourine, maintaining a firm and steady beat. Invite children to stride around with long steps and stamping feet, moving in time to the beats, such as slow, slow, quick, quick, quick. Play one instrument and then the other, swapping at random, and ask children to match movements to the sounds they hear.

Introduce a third instrument that makes a quick and distinctive sound, such as a drum or cymbals. Ask the children to jump and then freeze on the spot when they hear the bang or crash. Play the three instruments in a random order, encouraging children to make the three different movements, changing each time the instrument changes. Finish the game with a jump/freeze, asking children to think up interesting poses for their final 'freeze positions'.

Extensions/Variations
Ask children to suggest characters for each movement, such as fairies or cats tiptoeing, giants or giraffes striding and spiders or frogs jumping and freezing. Some children may prefer to think of vehicles, such as boats, buses or trains, moving gently and smoothly or noisily and jerkily, in time to a beat.

Support children in making hats, ears, wigs and other headdresses on cardboard headbands, using card or strips of paper. Ask the children to carry their headdresses and to put on the correct ones to match their character movements, swapping each time they change.

Play with a small seated group and give each child three instruments to play, that match those of the practitioner. Encourage them to copy, changing as soon as the leader changes.

Learning objectives/Early Learning Goals
* Notice changes in what is heard (CL–LA)
* Count beats and reproduce specific numbers of beats as necessary (M–N)
* Explore the different sounds of instruments and use them appropriately to enhance performances (EAD–EUMM)
* Move rhythmically and show awareness of tempo and mood (EAD–EUMM)
* Explore and learn how sounds can be changed (EAD–EUMM)
* Maintain attention and move or stop quietly when appropriate (CL–LA)
* Negotiate space successfully within a group (PD–MH)
* Portray characters and emotions through mime and expressive movement, understanding that the body can be used for communication (EAD–BI)
* Use available resources to create costume pieces and props to support role-play (EAD–BI)
* Improve confidence and social skills through participation in a large group activity (PSED–MR, MFB; PD–MH)

© Debbie Chalmers and Brilliant Publications

Chinese dragons

Themes
* Times Of Year/Celebrations
* Creatures/Animals/Birds/Plants
* Music/Sound

Skills
* Listening
* Movement/Dance
* Acting/Mime
* Confidence
* Group work
* Craftwork

Equipment/Resources
A safe, clear space in which children may move around easily; CD player; CD featuring some music suitable for a dragon dance (Chinese if possible); large pieces of brightly coloured fabric, tablecloths or throws, for costumes; craft materials and resources, including coloured papers and self-adhesive 'jewels'; staplers and staples, pens, sticky tape and scissors; percussion instruments and other items to make noises

Activity
Tell the story of the fierce dragon who lived in China a long time ago, frightening all the people and eating their vegetables and their animals. When they found out that the dragon didn't like loud noises, the Chinese people shouted and banged things together and set off fireworks to scare it away. At Chinese New Year, they remember the story and make big dragon costumes to dance in, hold parades in the streets to celebrate and set off fireworks.

Discuss and practise dragon movements with the children. Encourage them to decide when to move forwards, backwards or sideways, how many steps to take in each direction, when to pause or turn and how to stay together as a group to portray a long dragon's body

Support the children in making costumes to perform as dragons in small groups, stapling craft pieces to fabric and standing under it. Invite them to take turns to dance as a dragon, while the rest of the group uses instruments or other items to make loud noises.

Extensions/Variations
Invite the children's families and carers into the setting to watch the Chinese dragons perform their dances. Invite any Chinese family members into the setting to help and advise.

Support children in making small paper Chinese dragons, attached to straws with sticky tape, to use as stick puppets that they may move with their hands to create zigzag and undulating movements.

Provide a CD player and demonstrate how to use it safely, so that children may choose music and songs for themselves and create mimes during free play sessions.

Learning objectives/Early Learning Goals
* Listen to stories, songs or rhymes with increasing attention and recall, in order to discuss and recreate all or parts of them (CL–LA)
* Explore the different sounds of instruments and use them appropriately to enhance performances (EAD–EUMM)
* Move rhythmically and show awareness of tempo and mood (EAD–EUMM)
* Develop and act out a storyline or a narrative, working cooperatively within a group, and practise skills to perform before others with confidence (EAD–BI; PSED–SCSA)
* Gain an awareness of the cultures and beliefs of others (UW–PC)
* Use positional language, count steps and talk about distances and directions (UW–W)
* Use available resources to create costume pieces and props to support role-play (EAD–BI)
* Safely use and explore a variety of materials, tools and techniques, experimenting with colour, design, texture, form and function (EAD–EUMM)

What was that word?

Themes
* Stories/Fairy Tales
* Nursery Rhymes/Poems/Songs
* Food/Drinks/Meals

Skills
* Listening
* Confidence
* Movement/Dance

Equipment/Resources
A safe, clear space in which adults and children can sit together but in separate spaces; a read-aloud story with lots of repetition – published or home made

Activity
Gather the group together and invite them to play a listening game. Explain that they will need to sit as a group, but allow enough space between themselves to stand up and sit down without bumping each other. Practise with a simple rhyme, such as Incy Wincy Spider. Ask the children to stand up, turn around on the spot and sit down again every time they hear the word spider. Speak the rhyme clearly, slightly emphasizing the word each time you say spider and pausing if necessary to allow all children a chance to get up.

Once the group is confident, tell them the word to listen out for and then read the story with a steady rhythm, encouraging some children with hand signals if they forget when to stand up and don't copy the others. This game often causes much hilarity amongst young children, especially if you begin to gradually read a little more quickly towards the end of the story. You could write your own story to ensure that one or more particular words are repeated frequently enough.

Extensions/Variations
Divide the children into two or more smaller groups and give each group a different word to listen for. The resulting chaos, as they try to react only to their own word and not copy another group when they stand up, causes even more hilarity.

Give the children separate actions for two or three different words and challenge them not to muddle them up! For example, they could stand up, turn around and sit down for the first word, stand up, hop three times and sit down for the second word and stand up, wave their arms and sit down for the third word.

Ask the children to perform their action whenever they hear a word that rhymes with 'tree', or a word beginning with the sound 'b'.

Try the activity using recipes, as they are very repetitive and the names of foods and methods come up at random but frequently.

Learning objectives/Early Learning Goals
* Listen to stories, songs or rhymes with increasing attention and recall, in order to discuss and recreate all or parts of them (CL–LA)
* Notice changes in what is heard (CL–LA)
* Recognize rhythm, rhyme and alliteration and use them in activities (L–R)
* Improve confidence and social skills through participation in a large group activity (PSED–MR, MFB; PD–MH)
* Match movements and actions to the space available (PD–MH)
* Maintain attention, concentrate and move or stop quietly when appropriate (CL–LA)
* Learn and use the vocabulary of movement and controlled effort (PD–MH)

Cue for a rhyme

Themes
* Nursery Rhymes/Poems/Songs
* Music/Sound

Skills
* Listening
* Speech
* Confidence
* Group work

Equipment/Resources
A quiet place for a group of adults and children to sit, free from distractions; CD player; CD featuring children's rhymes and songs.

Activity
Invite the children to listen to a familiar nursery rhyme or simple song on a CD and to guess which one it is as quickly as they can (from the introduction or the opening bars).

Ask the children to join in and speak (not sing) the words in unison with an adult, who acts as a role model to encourage clear enunciation and a steady rhythm. Explain the words 'in unison' (all together at the same time) and 'enunciating' (speaking very clearly), as young children love to learn new words that sound interesting and 'grown up'. When they tell their families at home that they have been 'enunciating in unison', parents and carers will be very impressed with the quality of the drama teaching!

Tell the children that the adult is very forgetful and needs some help to get the words right, then say the rhyme, pausing at key words and waiting for the children to call them out. Each time they supply the correct words, move on to the next line and pause again to allow the children to supply the next key word.

Finally, repeat the rhyme together as a group, chanting clearly and steadily in unison. Thank the children for 'taking their cues' (coming in at the right time with the right words) and helping the adult to learn the rhyme.

Extensions/Variations
Instead of pausing, deliberately get key words wrong while saying the rhyme (eg Humpty Dumpty sat on a chair or Baa, baa, black sheep, have you any biscuits?), encouraging the children to shout 'No!' to stop the adult and call out the correct words. This is always a favourite and hilarious activity, that can be made gradually more and more challenging through careful choices of rhymes and substituted words (eg Incy Wincy spider climbed up the stairs to bed).

Ask children to supply whole lines of rhymes, rather than words (eg Row, row, row your boat – Gently down the stream – Merrily, merrily, merrily, merrily – Life is but a dream).

Demonstrate how to use the CD player and allow children to use it freely, to listen to rhymes and songs while playing, or to play the guessing game independently.

Learning objectives/Early Learning Goals
* Listen to stories, songs or rhymes with increasing attention and recall, in order to discuss and recreate all or parts of them (CL–LA)
* Join in with repeated refrains and anticipate key phrases in rhymes and songs (CL–LA)
* Take cues confidently to fill in the missing word or phrase in a known rhyme or song (L–R)
* Improve enunciation, in order to express words, ideas and messages clearly (CL–S)
* Speak clearly, both in unison and individually (CL–S; PSED–SCSA)
* Improve confidence and social skills through participation in a large group activity (PSED–MR, MFB, PD–MH)
* Operate simple technological equipment to allow repeated listening to songs, music, sounds or stories (UW–T)

Building a rhyme

Themes
* Nursery Rhymes/Poems/Songs
* Music/Sound

Skills
* Listening
* Speech
* Confidence
* Group work

Equipment/Resources
A quiet place for a group of adults and children to sit, free from distractions; CD player; CD featuring children's rhymes and songs.

Activity
Gather a group of practitioners and children together to sit in a circle. Choose a favourite rhyme or song together. Chant the words in unison, to ensure that everybody knows them all and to check any variations. For example, in I'm a Little Teapot, the third line can be: When I see the teacups or When I get the steam up or When the kettle's boiling. If different versions or verses are popular, decide as a group which line you will use, or decide in which order you will use them, one after another, repeating the rhyme more than once.

The leader should speak the first line of the rhyme clearly and ask each child and adult in turn to take a cue from the person next to them and continue with the next line. Each time somebody says the last line of the rhyme, the person next to them can begin again with the first line, to repeat the rhyme or introduce the next verse.

When each person in the circle has spoken, the leader can end the game by speaking the last lines to finish the rhyme, however many or few are left.

Extensions/Variations
Begin rhymes without choosing or announcing them first and invite children to supply the next line, one after another, spontaneously. It doesn't matter whether one child or many children call out each time. Include some very easy and familiar ones and some more challenging and less well known ones. Encourage confidence and praise all attempts, so that children are prepared to try and are not afraid of making mistakes.

Invite other practitioners and children to be the leader and to begin a rhyme for the group.

Demonstrate how to operate the CD player and allow children to choose CDs and play them freely, to listen, speak and sing along or dance.

Learning objectives/Early Learning Goals
* Listen to stories, songs or rhymes with increasing attention and recall, in order to discuss and recreate all or parts of them (CL–LA)
* Join in with repeated refrains and anticipate key phrases in rhymes and songs (CL–LA)
* Take cues confidently to fill in the missing word or phrase in a known rhyme or song (L–R)
* Improve enunciation, in order to express words, ideas and messages clearly (CL–S)
* Speak clearly, both in unison and individually (CL–S; PSED–SCSA)
* Improve confidence and social skills through participation in a large group activity (PSED–MR, MFB, PD–MH)
* Operate simple technological equipment to allow repeated listening to songs, music, sounds or stories (UW–T)

Follow that horse

Themes
* Creatures/Animals/Birds/Plants
* Times of Year/Celebrations

Skills
* Confidence
* Movement/Dance
* Acting/Mime
* Listening

Equipment/Resources
A clear, safe pathway around the setting, indoors or outdoors – or both; percussion instruments, including kazoos and drums or tambourines if possible; CD player; CDs featuring appropriate marching, parade or dance tunes

Activity
Explain that horses often perform in circuses and ask whether any of the children have seen them – live or on television. Tell them that circuses are often held at Christmas and other special times of year. Talk about how the horses follow each other around the ring in a line and 'dance' to music, while riders perform tricks on their backs. Discuss the types of music that they might move to and how it might be played by a live band.

Invite the children to form a line, one behind the other, and to follow a practitioner who will lead them all around the setting.

Encourage them to copy each of the horse-like movements made by the adult, which could

include: walking, trotting, galloping, prancing, nodding and shaking heads, sniffing the air, walking sideways, walking backwards and stopping.

Add horse sounds, such as neighing, snorting and blowing, for extra effect.

Provide any suitable marching or parading music or dance tunes played by a brass or jazz band for everybody to move to.

Extensions/Variations
Invite children to take turns to lead small groups and decide what the horses will do.

Ask children to listen to the words (adjectives) called out by a practitioner and change their horses' movements to fit. Try: quickly, slowly, loudly/noisily, quietly/softly, happily, crossly and tiredly/wearily.

Try making a line of dogs, elephants or monkeys and performing their movements instead.

Invite children to make their own band music with percussion instruments. Suggest that one group plays the music while another group dances and then they swap places.

Learning objectives/Early Learning Goals
* Understand a new concept and verbalize thinking and understanding (CL–U, S)
* Develop and use skills and explore concepts and ideas, embracing challenge and greater stimulation (EAD–BI)
* Lead a group confidently (PSED–SCSA, MR)
* Maintain attention, concentrate and move or stop quietly when appropriate (CL–LA)
* Interact as a member of a group to develop and act out a narrative or storyline through dance (EAD–BI)
* Listen carefully and imitate and create movements in response to types of music (EAD–EUMM, BI)
* Portray characters and emotions through mime and expressive movement, understanding that the body can be used for communication (EAD–BI)
* Explore the different sounds of instruments and use them appropriately to enhance performances (EAD–EUMM)

Life cycles

Themes
* Creatures/Animals/Birds/Plants
* Seasons/Weather/Elements

Skills
* Confidence
* Movement/Dance
* Acting/Mime
* Group work

Equipment/Resources
A safe, clear floor space in which children can move around easily; books, posters and Internet sources of information on sunflowers (and chickens, frogs, butterflies and other life cycles); small plant pots or plastic cups, soil and sunflower seeds; plastic spoons, small watering cans and lamps or torches music player; song: We've Grown so Tall (available to download from Brilliant Publications' website)

Activity
Use books, pictures, posters and educational or gardening websites to introduce the idea of planting seeds and growing sunflowers. Take the children out to see sunflowers growing in the outdoor area, a local garden, public place or garden centre. Discuss their uses as crops (eg to make cooking oils). Provide pots, soil, spoons, small watering cans and sunflower seeds and support children in planting seeds. Talk about what plants need to grow.

Invite children to pretend to be seeds, curled up in the soil, and to feel the sun and the rain and begin to grow. Encourage them to push out their arms and legs as 'spiky shoots' and to gradually grow upwards and stretch until they are waving in the sunshine. Introduce action songs to help the children to create movements, such as We've Grown so Tall.

Ask children to portray the sun and the rain symbolically (by spreading out their arms and wriggling their fingers in downwards movements), then to pretend to be the gardeners or farmers inspecting their flowers and to show whether they are pleased with them or not.

Offer the children lamps or torches that they can safely turn on and off independently and invite them to use them as 'the sun' that the flowers will grow towards. Create acts with small groups of children, involving some actors as the sun, some as the rain and some as growing sunflowers, then support them as they perform to each other.

Extensions/Variations
Plant the sunflower shoots outside. Measure, compare and describe them regularly.

Explore and act out other life cycles, such as those of the chicken, frog and butterfly.

Learning objectives/Early Learning Goals
* Understand a new concept and verbalize thinking and understanding (CL–U, S)
* Develop skills and explore ideas, embracing challenge and greater stimulation (EAD–BI)
* Initiate new combinations of movement to express feelings and ideas (EAD–BI)
* Learn and use the vocabulary of movement and controlled effort (PD–MH)
* Create simple representations of events and creatures to develop a watchable movement sequence within the boundaries of a given storyline or narrative (EAD–BI)
* Develop and act out an experience or a narrative, working cooperatively within a group, and practise skills to perform before others with confidence (EAD–BI; PSED–SCSA)
* Operate simple technological equipment for use in dramatic activities (UW–T)
* Confidently try a new activity and explore an unfamiliar theme (PSED–SCSA)
* Remember rules and aims of the activity and try various different strategies (PSED–MR, MFB)

© Debbie Chalmers and Brilliant Publications

Confidence

Order and direction

Themes
* People Who Help Us/Occupations
* Travelling/Places

Skills
* Confidence
* Acting/Mime
* Movement/Dance
* Group work

Equipment/Resources
A safe, clear space in which children can move around easily; hats or helmets suitable for police officers (full dressing-up outfits optional); wheeled toys, dolls and soft animals; chalk

Activity
Demonstrate for the children simple commands that a police officer might make when directing traffic, such as holding up a hand for 'Stop' and waving a hand in a beckoning motion for 'Go'. Ask the children if they recognize what the mimes mean and if they think drivers, cyclists and pedestrians would know what to do if they saw them. Explain that police officers direct traffic at junctions when traffic lights break down, around complicated roadworks and when there has been an accident. Ask if children can think of other signals that a police officer might make. For example, they might ask somebody to wait or direct a car to pull over and park in a particular place. Show that two actions may happen at once, when a police officer stops one line of traffic and tells another line to go.

Ask children to 'drive', cycle or walk around, obeying directions as traffic. If playing with a large group, two or three police officers could work simultaneously, each directing groups of people and vehicles. Remind the children of how to use wheeled toys safely and encourage them to take on the roles of police officers and lead the game for themselves.

Extensions/Variations
Mark out roads and junctions outside with chalk, and encourage children to create imaginative games involving police officers directing children riding wheeled toys and 'crossing the roads' with toy pushchairs and dolls or toy dogs on leads made from ribbons.

Talk about the health benefits of walking, rather than driving, when possible.

Invite a police officer to visit the setting and talk to the children about road safety and how they direct traffic on busy roads.

Learning objectives/Early Learning Goals
* Have an awareness of and an interest in jobs and occupations (UW–PC)
* Improve confidence and social skills through participation in a large group activity (PSED–MR, MFB; PD–MH)
* Share ideas within a group and develop imagination around a theme, showing sensitivity to others' needs and feelings and forming positive relationships (PSED–MR)
* Portray different characters through a variety of movements and actions (EAD–BI)
* Re-enact real, first-hand experiences through imaginative role play (EAD–BI)
* Negotiate space successfully within a group, adjusting speed or changing direction to avoid obstacles or collisions (PD–MH)
* Remember rules and aims of the game or activity and try various different strategies (PSED–MR, MFB)
* Follow instructions following several ideas or actions (CL–U)
* Follow simple safety rules, tackle new challenges and manage appropriate risks (PD–MH, HSC; PSED–SCSA)
* Know that physical exercise can contribute to good health (PD–HSC)

Jump up

Themes
* Ourselves/Bodies/Families
* Colours/Shapes/Numbers

Skills
* Confidence
* Movement/Dance
* Group work

Equipment/Resources
A safe, clear space in which adults and children can sit together comfortably in a group

Activity
Talk with the group about people's similarities and differences and how they make us interesting. Sit together as a group and play a game in which the children are invited to jump up when they hear a description that fits them and to sit down again when one doesn't apply.

Start simply with instructions such as: Jump up if you are a girl; jump up if you are a boy. Gradually move on to more complex and challenging ideas that require children to look carefully at themselves, to remember the recent past, to think about the future or to make links and connections with other parts of their lives. For example: Jump up if you are three; if you are wearing trousers; if you have red socks; if you had juice for breakfast today; if you are going home for lunch; if you like swimming; if your Mummy or Daddy works in an office; if your grandad drives a car.

Any child who needs extra support to participate can receive it from his key person, who will have knowledge of his home and family, likes and dislikes, in order to prevent confusion and to allow the game to continue for long enough to offer stimulation to those children who are enjoying the challenge.

Extensions/Variations
Use this game to reinforce knowledge and understanding of any topics that the group has been studying, such as colours, textures, materials, numbers, food, families, pets, ways of travelling to nursery or favourite animals or activities. For example: Jump up if your jumper is made of wool; if you have two brothers; if your family speaks Japanese; if you walked to nursery this morning; if you like cats.

Encourage children to learn and remember letters, sounds and phonics by playing the game with commands such as: Jump up if your name begins with the sound 'j'; if your name ends with the sound 'a'; if your name has a 't' sound in the middle.

Learning objectives/Early Learning Goals
* Have an awareness of and an interest in cultural and language differences or jobs and occupations (UW–PC)
* Develop and use skills and explore concepts and ideas, embracing challenge and greater stimulation (EAD–BI)
* Maintain attention, concentrate and move or stop quietly when appropriate (CL–LA)
* Develop good control and coordination in large and small movements (PD–MH)
* Participate in a large group game or activity, understanding the need for rules and cooperation to ensure everybody's enjoyment (PSED–MR, MFB)

Thank you for watching

Themes
* Ourselves/Bodies/Families
* Times of Year/Celebrations

Skills
* Confidence
* Acting/Mime
* Movement/Dance
* Group work

Equipment/Resources
A clear, safe space in which children can move around each other easily; music player; song: Click Your Fingers (available to download from Brilliant Publications' website); CD player and CDs featuring children's action songs and dance music

Activity
Demonstrate a basic bow and a simple curtsey and explain to the children that performers use these to indicate that they have reached the end and to thank their audiences. Ask them to think about how they are using their bodies to communicate and what they are saying. ('Now I have finished. Thank you for watching.' and also 'You can clap now!')

Invite children to try the simple bows and curtseys and then to think of different and interesting ways to bow or curtsey. They could make grand, sweeping gestures with their arms, take steps, spin, jump or pretend to be a particular character or animal.

Share action songs, such as Click Your Fingers, to give children new ideas, and then play the bowing game again.

Practitioners and children can bow as a group or in lines, in unison or individually, to an imaginary audience or to each other.

Ensure that both boys and girls feel comfortable about choosing either to bow or to curtsey or to try both. It's important not to be gender specific in the foundation stage, while children are learning from a wide range of experiences and opportunities.

Extensions/Variations
Try a simple version of a 'Mexican wave'. Form one long line (preferably with an adult at each end) and ask everybody to watch each other carefully. The person at one end of the line should bow and each person should begin to bow a second or two after the one next to him, until all are down together. The last person in the line should stand up again immediately after the bow and each person should follow a second or two later, so that the 'wave' returns to the first person, who stands up last.

Invite children to dance freely to music in pairs or small groups and to bow or curtsey to their partners before and after each dance.

Pause the music at frequent intervals, as in the game Musical Statues, and ask children to bow or curtsey in a different way each time it stops, before dancing again.

Learning objectives/Early Learning Goals
* Understand a new concept and verbalize thinking and understanding (CL–U, S)
* Improve confidence and social skills through participation in a large group activity (PSED–MR, MFB; PD–MH)
* Thank an audience after a performance through body language, without need for speech (EAD–BI)
* Move freely and with pleasure and confidence in a range of ways (PD–MH)
* Match movements and actions to the space available (PD–MH)
* Develop good control and coordination in large and small movements (PD–MH)
* Follow instructions involving several ideas or actions (CL–U)

What shall we wear?

Themes
* Colours/Shapes/Numbers
* Ourselves/Bodies/Families
* People Who Help Us/Occupations

Skills
* Confidence
* Group work
* Movement/Dance
* Acting/Mime

Equipment/Resources
A safe, clear space in which adults and children can move around easily; dressing-up outfits and accessories; string and clothes pegs; large die or spinner featuring six different colours or numbers 1–6

Activity
Stretch a length of string across the room and tie it securely at each side to furniture, equipment or door handles, etc. It should hang at around the children's chest levels or lower (not as high as their necks). Invite children to help you to peg up shirts, tunics, jackets, trousers, dresses, hats, gloves, scarves, belts and any other dressing up items available along the 'washing line'. Ensure that the garments are in a random order with colours, textures and types of clothing not grouped together.

Make a die from a square tissue box covered in white paper or a spinner from stiff card and a long paper fastener and decorate it on the six sides or in six sections with marker pens. Or use a commercially produced large die or spinner, or one that you have previously made.

Invite children to play a dressing up game. Younger children may take turns to throw the coloured die or spin the coloured spinner and take a garment that is completely or mostly that colour from the line and put it on. Older ones may throw the number die or spin the number spinner and count along the line, from left to right, to take the garment that matches the number and put it on. Encourage children to dress themselves and manage fastenings and to help each other to dress in garments when they are tricky. Ask each child to mime or act something that a person wearing that item or outfit might do. For example, a person with a police helmet might direct traffic or a person wearing a scarf might shiver and rub their hands together because they are outside in cold weather.

When all the garments have been taken from the line, ask children to count how many different items they are each wearing – and to think about how funny they all look!

Extensions/Variations
Suggest that children throw or spin for each other and choose garments for other players to wear.

Introduce the extra rule that a player must miss a turn if they throw or spin a colour or number that matches a type of garment that they are already wearing.

Learning objectives/Early Learning Goals
* Have an awareness of and an interest in cultural and language differences or jobs and occupations (UW–PC)
* Participate in a large group game or activity, understanding the need for rules and cooperation to ensure everybody's enjoyment (PSED–MR, MFB)
* Manage own personal needs successfully and offer help to others (PD–HSC)
* Initiate new combinations of movement and gesture to express and respond to feelings and ideas (EAD–BI)
* Portray characters and emotions through mime and expressive movement, understanding that the body can be used for communication (EAD–BI)

Building site

Themes
* Building/Homes
* Travelling/Places
* People Who Help Us/Occupations

Skills
* Confidence
* Movement/Dance
* Listening
* Speech
* Acting/Mime

Equipment/Resources
A safe, clear space in which adults and children can move around easily; non-fiction books about machines and building; fiction books such as the stories of Bob the Builder by Diane Redmond (BBC Worldwide); CD player; CDs featuring Bob the Builder songs and other children's building songs; instrumental track: London Bridge (available to download from Brilliant Publications' website)

Activity
Gather the group together and discuss the types of machines that work on a building site and what they do. Children may suggest diggers, cranes, dumper trucks, cement mixers, rollers and fork lifts. Share non-fiction books with pictures of machines at work.

Move into spaces and mime the actions of the various machines, such as moving forward and back, spinning around and using arms to bend, lift, carry, swing or scoop.

Encourage children also to talk and work together in pairs and groups to create mimes or acts, with narration or dialogue, such as a crane lifting poles and dropping them into a dumper truck to be driven away, a digger scooping up sand and emptying its bucket into a mixer which spins the sand around or builders giving directions to each other or their machines. If they are creating a story, rather than a realistic sequence, they may choose to give the machines different voices too to allow them to speak to each other or talk about what they need to do. Invite children to add sound effects to their acts.

Extensions/Variations
Talk with children about what they might build, such as houses, offices, schools, shops or bridges. Encourage them to listen to and sing along with appropriate songs as they build, or to sing favourite action songs on the theme of building at group times. Use songs such as: Build it Up, I'm Going to Build a Little House and London Bridge.

Read stories about building and machines and lead children in acting them out, encouraging them to join in, copy, offer ideas to the group and make up actions of their own.

(If possible, obtain some Bob the Builder episodes on DVD to watch and discuss.)

Learning objectives/Early Learning Goals
* Think independently and offer ideas confidently to a group (PSED–SCSA; CL–S)
* Have an awareness of jobs and occupations (UW–PC)
* Improve confidence and social skills through participation in a large group activity (PSED–MR, MFB; PD–MH)
* Move freely and with pleasure and confidence in a range of ways (PD–MH)
* Listen to stories, songs or rhymes with increasing attention and recall, in order to discuss and recreate all or parts of them (CL–LA)
* Use language to imagine and recreate ideas and experiences for acting and role play (CL–S)
* Use talk to organize, sequence and clarify thinking, ideas, feelings and events when planning scenarios or performances (CL–S)
* Work cooperatively with others to act out a familiar part of a storyline (EAD–BI)
* Explore and develop skills of characterization within a small group, using different forms and language and intonation to imagine and recreate roles and experiences (CL–S)

Tree directions

Themes
* Seasons/Weather/Elements
* Creatures/Animals/Birds/Plants
* Colours/Shapes/Numbers

Skills
* Confidence
* Movement/Dance
* Acting/Mime
* Group work

Equipment/Resources
A safe, clear floor space in which children can move around easily

Activity
Adults stand in spaces, pretending to be trees in a forest, allowing enough room between them for children to move around safely and comfortably. They take turns to call out simple instructions that the children can follow, such as "Four people stand behind each tree" or 'Crawl around a tree three times' or 'Make a long line and walk between the trees'. Assuming that the adults are not all identical, give instructions such as: 'The wind blows you into spinning circles around a tree with long hair' or 'Sit in the sunshine in a ring around a tree with blue trousers' or 'Shelter from the rain by standing under the tallest tree.'

Children may play the game as themselves or as other characters, or pretend to be animals, birds, mini-beasts or mythical monsters, following each direction in turn and changing whenever they hear a new one.

To end the game, an adult can call out, 'Curl up in front of a tree and sleep for a hundred years!' When all the children are 'sleeping', the 'trees' can tiptoe away and say to each other that they will go home now and come back after a hundred years! The children usually spring up in alarm and then enjoy the joke.

Extensions/Variations
Ask children to take turns to follow directions, moving two or three at a time rather than as a whole group.

Offer two or three directions as a sequence, rather than single ones (eg jump to one tree, run around two trees, then stand in front of a different tree and count to ten).

Invite half of the children to be the trees in the forest, while the others move around, and support them as they play the game by themselves.

Play the game moving as animals, or pretending to be in a desert, a swamp, a jungle or an arctic wasteland, or swimming through the ocean.

Learning objectives/Early Learning Goals
* Improve confidence and social skills through participation in a large group activity (PSED–MR, MFB; PD–MH)
* Develop and use skills and explore concepts and ideas, embracing challenge and greater stimulation (EAD–BI)
* Match movements and actions to the space available (PD–MH)
* Develop good control and coordination in large and small movements (PD–MH)
* Learn and use the vocabulary of movement and controlled effort (PD–MH)
* Maintain concentration and participation in a large group activity and cooperate in a game that requires turn-taking and understanding of rules (PSED–MR, MFB)
* Follow instructions involving several ideas and actions (CL–U)
* Count aloud reliably using numbers 1–10 or 1–20 in order while playing a group game, to make a number of steps or jumps, or people in a group, or to wait for a number of seconds (M–N)
* Use positional language, count steps and talk about distances and directions (UW–W)

Hungry snake

Themes
* Creatures/Animals/Birds/Plants
* Seasons/Weather/Elements
* Food/Drinks/Meals

Skills
* Group work
* Acting/Mime
* Movement/Dance

Equipment/Resources
A clear space to work in with a safe, clean floor or ground surface

Activity
Explain that mime is acting without talking or making any sounds at all. Suggest to the children that they could pretend to be a creature that makes no sound and show everybody which creature they are and what they are doing through movement and mime. One practitioner needs to speak, to tell the story, but others can join in with the mime to encourage the children and to model interesting and appropriate movements and reactions.

The story could be similar to this:

Imagine that you are hungry snakes in the jungle or rainforest, looking for food. You slither along on the ground, looking all around. You see a lizard basking in the hot sun and slide up to it, but it scuttles down a hole in the sand and you have to slide away quickly because the sand is too hot. You see a spider in a web and slide up to it, but it climbs up a thread and out of reach. You try to stretch up to reach it, but fall down again.

Imagine that the rain now starts to fall heavily and the snakes slither quickly up trees to shelter in the leaves and look for food. You see a monkey and begin to coil around it, but it swings away through the trees and you hang from the branch instead. You see a sloth hanging upside down and begin to coil around it, but it pulls itself away along a branch and you can't reach it. You see a bat hanging with its wings down and begin to coil around it, but it swings itself up to stand and flaps away. You hide from its wings, under the branch. At last, you smell some insects coming out of their nest under the branch. You dart out your forked tongue and eat some!

Extensions/Variations
Ask the children to pretend to be each of the different creatures in turn, thinking about their movements, speeds and reactions. Then invite children to choose which creature they will be and encourage one or more to represent each one, while some continue to be snakes, as they act out the scenario again.

Learning objectives/Early Learning Goals
* Follow treasure hunts or trails in character, exploring an outdoor or indoor area as an animal or a person from a story (UW–W; EAD–EUMM)
* Portray characters and emotions through mime and expressive movement, understanding that the body can be used for communication (EAD–BI)
* Create simple representations of events, people, creatures or objects to develop a watchable movement sequence within the boundaries of a given storyline or narrative (EAD–BI)
* Initiate new combinations of movement and gesture to express and respond to feelings and ideas (EAD–BI)
* Develop good control and coordination in large and small movements (PD–MH)

Follow the trail

Themes
* Creatures/Animals/Birds/Plants
* Travelling/Places
* Stories/Fairy Tales

Skills
* Group work
* Acting/Mime
* Movement/Dance
* Craftwork

Equipment/Resources
A clear space in which adults and children can move around easily and safely; picture books involving journeys: *We're Going on a Bear Hunt* by Michael Rosen and Helen Oxenbury (Walker Books Ltd), *Bears in the Night* by Stan and Jan Berenstain (Harper Collins) and *Where the Wild Things Are* by Maurice Sendak (Harper Collins); large pieces of card and rolls of frieze paper, natural resources and collage materials; paper, glue, sticky tape, scissors and pencils or pens; programmable toy, such as a Roamer or a Beebot

Activity
Read popular stories involving people or animals going on journeys and talk with the children about ways of moving and travelling and different environments. Act out the stories, including lots of different movements, such as: running, climbing, wading, swimming, squeezing, crawling and rolling. Imagine that you are moving through different terrains, such as: woods, paths, long grass, mud, hills, bridges and water. Move as people, bears, monsters, mini-beasts or any other creatures that the children are interested in.

Set up trails for the children to follow outside, using trees, tyres, planks, climbing frames, tunnels, etc. Encourage them to climb, balance, crawl, wriggle through gaps and jump down, in character. Ensure that trails are challenging enough for individual children; supervise them closely, but encourage them to manage their own safety without avoiding all risks. Support children as they move equipment around to plan and make their own trails and obstacle courses. Talk about healthy physical exercise, taking risks and keeping safe.

Extensions/Variations
Offer 'treasure', such as snacks, toys or play money, for children to include in their games. Invite them to hide it at the end of a trail or give clues for others to find it.

Make pictures or friezes of trails or journeys with collage materials and natural resources such as leaves and twigs. Use them as 'set' pieces to create scenery for re-enacting stories.

Support children in drawing and writing their own travelling stories to make into books.

Provide a programmable toy and support children in making it follow a path or a set of instructions and directions. Talk about travelling in cars, buses, trains, boats and aeroplanes.

Learning objectives/Early Learning Goals
* Follow treasure hunts or trails in character, exploring an outdoor or indoor area as an animal or a person from a story (UW–W; EAD–EUMM)
* Follow simple safety rules, tackle new challenges and manage appropriate risks (PD–MH, HSC; PSED–SCSA)
* Know that physical exercise can contribute to good health (PD–HSC)
* Work cooperatively with others to act out a familiar part of a storyline (EAD–BI)
* Operate simple technological equipment for use in dramatic activities (UW–T)
* Move freely and with pleasure and confidence in a range of ways (PD–MH)
* Understand that different media can be combined to create new effects (EAD–EUMM)
* Use skills to explore concepts and ideas through representations (EAD–EUMM)

Corners

Themes
* Ourselves/Bodies/Families
* Colours/Shapes/Numbers
* Creatures/Animals/Birds/Plants

Skills
* Group work
* Movement/Dance

Equipment/Resources
A room with a clear space in the centre and in each corner in which adults and children can stand together and room to safely run between them; five or more practitioners – one to call out instructions and one for each corner

Activity
Ask a practitioner to stand in each corner of the room and gather the group of children in the centre. Invite them to play a group listening and movement game in which they will run to a particular corner if they match the description called out. Remind them to take care when running, to focus on where they are going and to avoid others who are moving at the same time.

Use simple instructions at first and the names of the four practitioners in the corners. For example: 'People with long hair run to Vicky! People wearing blue trousers run to Greg!' Encourage children still standing in the centre to remind those who do not run if they can see that they do match the descriptions.

Move on to less obvious instructions, that require children to link other experiences from their lives, rather than just looking at themselves, such as: 'If you have a dog at home, run to Tess! If your family has a red car, run to Andy!'

When children are confident about playing the game, use more complex instructions that ask them to make decisions or offer opinions and preferences, such as: 'People who like ice cream run to Debbie! If you think the sky is blue today, run to David!'

Invite children to run as different characters or creatures or as though they are driving vehicles or escaping from monsters. They could use sounds and expressions (but discourage any screaming).

Extensions/Variations
Instead of using the practitioners' names, give each corner the name of a colour, a shape or a number for children to remember, but ask the adults to stay in the corners to supervise the children and help them to run and stop safely.

Ask children to make different movements instead of running. For example: 'If you have two brothers, hop to the red corner! If you like cheese sandwiches, skip to the triangle corner! Everybody jump like a kangaroo to the number four corner!'

Learning objectives/Early Learning Goals
* Participate in a large group game or activity, understanding the need for rules and cooperation to ensure everybody's enjoyment (PSED–MR, MFB)
* Follow instructions involving several ideas or actions (CL–U)
* Follow simple safety rules, tackle new challenges and manage appropriate risks (PD–MH, HSC; PSED–SCSA)
* Negotiate space successfully within a group, adjusting speed or changing direction to avoid obstacles or collisions (PD–MH)
* Move freely and with pleasure and confidence in a range of ways (PD–MH)
* Portray different characters through a variety of movements and actions (EAD–BI)

Animal patterns

Themes
* Colours/Shapes/Numbers
* Creatures/Animals/Birds/Plants

Skills
* Group work
* Listening
* Movement/Dance
* Singing

Equipment/Resources
A clear space with a safe, clean floor or ground surface, in which adults and children can move around safely and easily

Activity
Speak to children individually, telling them each the name of an animal or creature and asking them all to keep their animals secret. Ask them to think about and practise their animals' movements.

Play a game in which you call out a colour and every child whose animal is or could be that colour mimes its movements, while everybody else 'freezes' to watch. For example, if you call out 'green', there might be a swimming crocodile, a sliding caterpillar and a running lizard; if you call out 'brown', a dog, a horse, a cow, a bear, a rabbit and many others will move; if you call out 'pink', there may be only a pig. Even colours such as red and blue can apply to butterflies and mini-beasts. Some creatures, such as snakes, frogs or spiders, could be almost any colour.

Repeat the activity using shapes and patterns instead of colours. You could include animals with spots, such as leopards and dogs, patches, such as giraffes and cows, and stripes, such as cats, tigers, zebras and snakes.

Extensions/Variations
Call out a number as well as a colour, shape or pattern and ask children to make, for example, five jumps or twelve gallops.

Sing and act out action and finger rhymes and songs involving colours and numbers, such as Ten Green Bottles and Five Little Speckled Frogs. (Tune available as an instrumental recording – track 10 on CD *J'aime Chanter* – Brilliant Publications.)

Learning objectives/Early Learning Goals
* Follow instructions involving several ideas or actions (CL–U)
* Participate in a large group game or activity, understanding the need for rules and cooperation to ensure everybody's enjoyment (PSED–MR, MFB)
* Count aloud reliably using numbers 1–10 or 1–20 in order while playing a group game, to make a number of steps or jumps or to wait for a number of seconds (M–N)
* Observe silences as part of a group, following agreed ideas and rules (PSED–MFB)
* Portray different characters through a variety of movements and actions (EAD–BI)
* Accurately anticipate and join in with repeated refrains and key phrases in songs, or respond with relevant actions (CL–LA)
* Confidently use songs and rhymes that involve number names, counting on and counting back in ones, twos, fives and tens, using fingers or whole body actions (M–N)

Roll the dice

Themes
* Colours/Shapes/Numbers
* Creatures/Animals/Birds/Plants

Skills
* Group work
* Movement/Dance
* Acting/Mime
* Craftwork

Equipment/Resources
A clear space to work in with a safe, clean floor or ground surface; empty square tissue boxes; white paper; PVA glue and spreaders or sticky tape; black marker pens and scissors

Activity
Cut the white paper into squares to fit and cover all six sides of each tissue box. Make one box into a number die, either with numerals 1–6 or with the appropriate spots, by drawing them with a black marker pen.

Make another box into a picture die by drawing animals and birds on the six sides. (The drawings can be very simple outlines or just symbolic representations, as long as the children can recognize them.) Choose those that make particular and different movements, such as frogs, horses, snakes, mice, owls and penguins.

Gather the group of children together. Roll the two dice and encourage children to call out what they have landed on. Ask them to make the animal's or bird's movement the correct number of times. For example, they may need to make three frog jumps,

two horse gallops or six penguin waddles.

Extensions/Variations
Make a third box into a shape die by drawing clear 2D shapes on the six sides. You might choose a circle, a square, a rectangle, a triangle, a star and a hexagon, or any shapes that the children are familiar with, or that you would like them to learn. Roll the die and ask children to make the shape it lands on with their bodies, cooperating to form shapes in pairs or small groups when necessary. The easiest way is to lie on the floor, but encourage inventiveness!

Stick six different coloured paper squares onto the six sides of another box to make a colour die. Invite children to divide themselves into six smaller groups or teams, each with one or more practitioners, and to give each team a different colour name to represent one side of the die. Use the colour die in conjunction with any of the other dice. Roll two dice to create instructions such as: Red team waddle like penguins; Blue team jump five times; Yellow team make a circle. Roll three dice to make up: Green team make six frog jumps or Orange team wriggle like snakes and make a square.

Learning objectives/Early Learning Goals
* Follow instructions involving several ideas or actions (CL–U)
* Count aloud or recognize numbers reliably while playing a group game, to make a number of steps or jumps or to wait a number of seconds (M–N)
* Portray different characters through a variety of movements and actions (EAD–BI)
* Develop good control and coordination in large and small movements (PD–MH)
* Create simple representations of events, people, creatures or objects (EAD–BI)
* Maintain concentration and participation in a large group activity and co-operate in a game that requires turn taking and understanding of rules (PSED–MR, MFB)

Beehives

Themes
* Building/Homes
* Colours/Shapes/Numbers

Skills
* Group work
* Movement/Dance
* Craftwork

Equipment/Resources
A clear space with a safe, clean floor surface, in which adults and children can move around easily and sit comfortably; coloured hoops – two or more in each of three or more different colours; CD player; CD featuring children's music or songs; large pieces of card and fabric; string, ribbon and elastic; scissors, staplers and sticky tape

Activity
Scatter hoops on the floor, leaving gaps between them. Invite children to 'fly' and 'buzz' around the room as bees, between the beehives, while music plays and freeze when it stops.

Stop the music at intervals and call out a number, such as: 'Six bees go home!' Encourage all children to run to the hoops and sit inside them together, making exactly six bees in each hoop. Encourage children to huddle together to squeeze into the hoops when necessary, like small bees tightly packed into their hives.

Repeat the activity with different numbers. Practitioners need to supervise, support and be available to join a group or drop out as necessary

to make up the correct number of players for each number.

Extensions/Variations
Make the game more challenging by calling out, for example: 'Five bees in the blue homes; three bees in the red homes!'

When the bees are in their hoops, ask them to use their bodies to build their homes in different shapes, such as tall thin beehives, tiny beehives or wobbly beehives.

Support children in making wings and cloaks that they can wear to help them to 'fly' as bees.

Learning objectives/Early Learning Goals
* Participate in a large group game or activity, understanding the need for rules and cooperation to ensure everybody's enjoyment (PSED–MR, MFB)
* Remember rules and aims of the game or activity and try various different strategies (PSED–MR, MFB)
* Follow instructions involving several ideas or actions (CL–U)
* Describe sizes, positions, distances or times through participating in group or ring games (M–SSM)
* Maintain attention, concentrate and move or stop quietly when appropriate (CL–LA)
* Negotiate space successfully within a group, adjusting speed or changing direction to avoid obstacles or collisions (PD–MH)
* Match movements and actions to the space available (PD–MH)
* Use available resources to create costume pieces and props to support role-play (EAD–BI)

Magic rings

Themes
* Music/Sound
* Ourselves/Bodies/Families
* Stories/Fairy Tales

Skills
* Group work
* Singing
* Movement/Dance
* Confidence

Equipment/Resources
A clear space in which adults and children can move around easily and safely as a group or in a circle

Activity
Research ring and group games and build up a collection, asking for ideas and contributions from other practitioners, parents and children. Include old favourites that are songs with actions, such as Ring a Ring a Roses, Here We Go Round the Mulberry Bush and Farmer's in his Den, more complicated songs and movement routines, such as In and Out the Dusty Bluebells and Round and Round the Village, story song ring games, such as There Was a Princess Long Ago and games in other formations that are either sung or chanted, as in Oranges and Lemons and What's the Time Mr Wolf?

Regularly play ring and other group games with a large group of children and as many practitioners as possible. Use the tunes and circular or forward motions to keep everybody together, adapting words and movements to suit any themes or ideas. Encourage children to chant numbers in unison, to walk around, go under, between or through, or stand behind each other, to act out characters and objects of various sizes, to move different distances and to represent times with numbers of steps or seconds, as appropriate to the game.

Extensions/Variations
Talk with children about the benefits of physical exercise and how vigorous but controlled movement can contribute to good health. Encourage them to play group and ring games during free play sessions, both with and without the support of practitioners, choosing and organising the games for themselves. Explain that playing such games, as well as racing and chasing games and running and climbing activities, are especially suitable for outdoor play and especially beneficial when played outside in the fresh air.

As a game progresses, encourage children to try to remember who has not yet had a turn and to choose partners and players with sensitivity, supporting them as much as necessary.

Learning objectives/Early Learning Goals
* Count aloud reliably using numbers 1–10 or 1–20 in order while playing a group game to make a number of steps or jumps or to wait for a number of seconds (M–N)
* Describe sizes, positions, distances or times through participating in group or ring games (M–SSM)
* Know that physical exercise can contribute to good health (PD–HSC)
* Participate in a large group game or activity, understanding the need for rules and cooperation to ensure everybody's enjoyment (PSED–MR, MFB)
* Explore and develop skills of characterization within a small group, by representing own ideas, thoughts and feelings through music, dance and role-play while acting out a familiar storyline within a song (EAD–BI)
* Match movements and actions to the space available (PD–MH)
* Work, speak and listen appropriately as a member of a group, showing sensitivity to others' needs and feelings and responding with consideration (PSED–MR)

Where should I be?

Themes
* Travelling/Places
* Colours/Shapes/Numbers
* Ourselves/Bodies/Families

Skills
* Group work
* Acting/Mime
* Movement/Dance

Equipment/Resources
A clear space in a room in which adults and children can sit together comfortably in a group and move around safely and easily; basic furniture around the sides of the room, such as tables, chairs and cupboards or screens

Activity
Ask each child by name to go to a particular place in the room. Include lots of positional and body language. Use your knowledge of individual children to ensure that they all understand the particular instructions they are given. Some will need to be simpler and others more challenging, but, provided that they are able to watch each other's movements from their positions, they will gradually absorb and understand more and more as the game progresses. For example: Could you kneel under a table? Please sit on a chair. Could you stand behind a cupboard? Please lie down in front of a screen.

When all of the children are in different positions, ask them to move around by giving further instructions such as: Crawl out from under the table and hop over to stand behind a chair. Please stand up and jump over to stand in front of a cupboard. Creep out from behind the cupboard and go to sit beside a screen. Please jump up and run over to touch a table.

Extensions/Variations
Play with smaller groups and give several instructions at once, such as: Three people under a table, two people on chairs and three people behind a screen. Ask the children to decide amongst themselves who will go where in order to fulfil the request and to check that they are right when they are all in position.

Add more character acting by asking children to hide under a table like a mouse or jump around a chair like a kangaroo or hide behind a screen and pop out like a jack-in-a-box!

Learning objectives/Early Learning Goals
* Follow instructions involving several ideas or actions (CL–U)
* Use positional language, count steps and talk about distances and directions (UW–T)
* Describe sizes, positions, distances or times through participating in group or ring games (M–SSM)
* Portray characters and emotions through mime and expressive movement, understanding that the body can be used for communication (EAD–BI)
* Maintain concentration and participation in a large group activity and cooperate in a game that requires turn taking and understanding of rules (PSED–MR, MFB)
* Move freely and with pleasure and confidence in a range of ways (PD–MH)
* Match movements and actions to the space available (PD–MH)
* Learn and use the vocabulary of movement and controlled effort (PD–MH)

Rainbow dance

Themes
* Seasons/Weather/Elements
* Colours/Shapes/Numbers

Skills
* Group work
* Movement/Dance
* Listening
* Singing

Equipment/Resources
A safe, clear space in which children can move around easily; long ribbons (or strips of fabric or chiffon scarves) in assorted colours, attached to short wooden sticks; CD player; CDs featuring children's songs about rainbows, weather and colours

Activity
Hand out ribbons to half of the children (or to a small group if you have fewer ribbons). Ask those without ribbons to sit down in spaces. Play the music and invite the children with ribbons to move around the space and sing and dance freely, making sweeping and swirling patterns around the seated children. Ask them to make shapes in the air, swirling the ribbons to create circles, squares and triangles that the other children can recognize. Encourage them to count how many circles they can make before they become dizzy or how many times they can wave the ribbon overhead before their arms are too tired.

Stop the music suddenly and ask the dancers to immediately give the ribbons to children who don't have them and sit down in spaces themselves. Start the music again for those who now have ribbons to dance. Each time the music stops, dancers should swap with seated children, until everybody has had several turns to dance. Those seated can sing along.

Extensions/Variations
Give a ribbon to each child (play with a smaller group if necessary), and call out a colour at intervals, instead of stopping and starting the music. Ask children to sit down when the colour of their ribbon is called out and then to stand up and carry on dancing when their colour is called again. (Have a number of identical ribbons in each colour and at least four different colours.)

Encourage all of the children to stand in a line, one behind the other, and to join in with the chant of 'One, two, three - rainbow!' As they say the last word, they can flick their ribbons in an arch over their heads together, to form a rainbow.

Learning objectives/Early Learning Goals
* Participate in a large group game or activity, understanding the need for rules and cooperation to ensure everybody's enjoyment (PSED–MR, MFB)
* Listen carefully and imitate and create movement in response to types of music (EAD–EUMM, BI)
* Negotiate space successfully within a group, adjusting speed or changing direction to avoid obstacles or collisions (PD–MH)
* Notice changes in what is heard (CL–LA)
* Listen to songs and sing back what is heard (EAD–EUMM)
* Memorize simple songs, including words, tunes and appropriate actions, and sing them in unison with others, maintaining a steady speed and volume (EAD–EUMM)

Portraits

Themes
* Colours/Shapes/Numbers
* Ourselves/Bodies/Families

Skills
* Craftwork
* Confidence
* Speech

Equipment/Resources
A clear space in which adults and children can work together comfortably as a group; large sheets of white paper and mirrors; paints and brushes in various colours, including skin tones and black and white; music player; songs: I've Got One Head and Toes and Knees (available to download from Brilliant Publications' website); CD player and CDs featuring Barney the Dinosaur (optional)

Activity
Gather practitioners and children together and ask them to look at each other and to think about similarities and differences between people. Invite them to look into mirrors to see themselves. Talk about clothes, shoes, sizes, hair, features and skin colours, as well as additions to appearances, such as wearing glasses. Invite children also to talk about and describe their families and friends. Ensure that every aspect is mentioned in a positive way.

Invite children and practitioners to paint pictures of themselves. Support the children in choosing the right colours, or mixing them if necessary, adding tiny amounts of black or white to adjust shades. Talk about the shapes of different facial features, hair, limbs and clothes and how many eyes, noses, mouths, ears, arms and legs to paint. Write the name of the artist on the back of each painting.

When the paintings are dry, lay them out upside down on the floor. Play some music and ask each child to pick up one and walk around with it, pretending to hold a conversation with the person in the picture. Stop the music and ask everybody to find the person in their painting and give it to them. (If some practitioners or children are not present when you play, take their pictures out of the pile before spreading them out.) Encourage players to help each other to recognize the portraits.

Extensions/Variations
Ask children to take portraits from a pile in turn, to see who their partners will be. The pairs can then sit together to practise conversation and dialogue, talking about the ways in which they are similar and the ways in which they are different.

Share songs such as I've Got One Head and Toes and Knees. Many songs about families and friends by Barney the Dinosaur could also be useful.

If children are older, confident or experienced, offer some simple conflict scenarios (such as both wanting to use the same pencil or wanting to have a snack together and finding only one seat free at the table) and ask them to talk about how they might solve the problems.

Learning objectives/Early Learning Goals
* Explore and experiment to create different colours or textures (EAD–EUMM)
* Use skills to explore concepts and ideas through representations (EAD–EUMM)
* Celebrate diversity, avoiding stereotypes and challenging any negative attitudes (UW–PC)
* Use and name shapes appropriately in creative tasks (M–SSM)
* Improve confidence and social skills through participation in a large group activity (PSED–MR, MFB; PD–MH)
* Explain own knowledge and understanding, ask appropriate questions of others, take account of others' ideas and resolve conflicts through compromise (PSED–MR)

© Debbie Chalmers and Brilliant Publications

A meal out

Themes
* Food/Drinks/Meals
* Colours/Shapes/Numbers
* People Who Help Us/Occupations

Skills
* Craftwork
* Acting/Mime

Equipment/Resources
A clear space in which adults and children can work together comfortably as a group; paper plates and plastic cups; white and coloured card and paper; coloured tissue paper; felt and fabric pieces Assorted craft pieces, including buttons, string, wool, stickers, pipe cleaners and straws; scissors, glue, spreaders and sticky tape; coloured pens and pencils; notepads; tills and play money; magazines with pictures of food to cut out

Activity
Invite children to cut out pieces and stick items together to create meals on paper plates. They could choose to make their favourite meals, foods they often eat at home or at nursery or school, foods that they don't like, or foods that they've never tasted.

Encourage them also to make drinks, using coloured paper, tissue paper or fabric stuck into plastic cups. They could attach a drinking straw to make a drink look more real.

Talk with the children as you work alongside them, naming and discussing the colours and shapes of the foods and drinks that everybody is creating and counting out how many peas, beans, tomatoes, chips, potatoes, fishfingers or sausages are on a plate.

When the meals are finished, invite the children to sit in a circle and to pretend to eat from their plates. Suggest different feelings, such as enjoying favourite foods, trying new tastes or disliking one of the foods, and ask the children to make expressions to show those feelings.

Extensions/Variations
Lay out the plates in the role play area and set out some tables and chairs to create a restaurant or café. Invite children to take turns to be waiters/waitresses or customers and to speak to each other politely, to request different foods and to find the right ones and serve them. Talk about the importance of washing hands before eating or handling food and of good hygiene practices in restaurants, cafés and kitchens.

Provide notepads and pencils, for waiters/waitresses to write down orders, numbers of customers and bills, and tills and play money so that customers can pay. Some children may also choose to make menus, using a combination of words and pictures.

Learning objectives/Early Learning Goals
* Explore and experiment to create different colours or textures (EAD–EUMM)
* Use and name shapes appropriately in creative tasks (M–SSM)
* Explore and develop skills of characterization within a small group, using different forms of language and intonation to imagine and recreate roles and experiences (CL–S)
* Share ideas within a group and develop imagination around a theme, showing sensitivity to others' needs and feelings and forming positive relationships (PSED–MR)
* Manage own basic personal and hygiene needs successfully (PD–HSC)
* Handle equipment and tools effectively, including pencils for drawing and writing (PD–MH)
* Use identifiable letters and phonic knowledge to communicate meaning (L–W)

Special times

Themes
* Food/Drinks/Meals
* Times Of Year/Celebrations
* Ourselves/Bodies/Families

Skills
Craftwork
Confidence
Speech
Acting/Mime

Equipment/Resources
A clear space in which adults and children can work together comfortably as a group; books, Internet resources and/or visitors to detail special occasion meals from various different cultures, faiths and communities; paper plates, plastic serving bowls and plastic cups; card and paper, tissue paper, felt and fabric pieces in assorted colours; assorted craft pieces, including buttons, string, wool, stickers, pipe cleaners and straws; scissors, glue, spreaders and sticky tape; coloured pens and pencils

Activity
Discuss with the children their experiences of special meals with their families for special occasions, such as birthdays, Christmas, Diwali, Hanukkah, Eid, Easter, New Year and Thanksgiving. Show pictures and provide items for them to handle, smell and taste. Invite family members or other community figures into the setting to talk about their special meals and, if possible, to bring in some food items to show to the children or to cook simple recipes with small groups or as a demonstration.

Invite children to recreate the meals with craft resources and found and recycled materials and to put the items into the serving bowls, then to sit around a table with a plate each and to serve themselves with the pretend food, observing whichever other customs are appropriate to the culture or faith that traditionally eats the meal.

Explain that people travel all over the world now and often live in countries other than the one they were born in. Restaurants serve foods from many countries and we are encouraged to be adventurous and to try new tastes. This means that most people eat all kinds of food and understand many different cultures and events, but they still enjoy following their own traditions at certain times of the year and eating the foods that symbolize the occasions for them.

Extensions/Variations
Invite parents to bring in photographs of their children taking part in special family events and occasions and ask if you may photocopy and return them, to use the copies in a scrapbook or display. Count with the children how many different experiences the group can record between them and encourage the view that it is interesting to find out about other people's beliefs and customs and to compare them with our own, as they can be so different but are all equally valid and important.

Learning objectives/Early Learning Goals
* Use media and materials in original ways to suit different uses of purposes (EAD–BI)
* Safely use and explore a variety of materials, tools and techniques, experimenting with colour, design, texture, form and function (EAD–EUMM)
* Celebrate diversity, avoiding stereotypes and challenging any negative attitudes (UW–PC)
* Gain an awareness of the cultures and beliefs of others (UW–PC)
* Talk about and explain the symbolic use of objects in pretend situations and as props (CL–S)
* Re-enact real, first-hand experiences through imaginative role-play (EAD–BI)

Hide and seek

Themes
* Building/Homes
* Creatures/Animals/Birds/Plants

Skills
* Craftwork
* Movement/Dance
* Group work
* Acting/Mime
* Listening

Equipment/Resources
A clear space with a safe, clean floor surface, in which adults and children can move around easily and sit comfortably; large construction blocks, made from plastic, foam or wood; tambourine

Activity
Ask each child, or group of up to four children, to build a wall to hide behind. It need not be very tall or wide, but they should be hidden when they sit or crouch behind it. (Unless you have a very large quantity of blocks you will need to play this game with small groups of children, or you could consider using tables turned sideways, large beanbags and floor cushions or cardboard boxes.) Explain that they are now in their dens and they might creep out.

Invite the children to creep out as mice, to scurry around to search for food and to creep back into the dens. Ask them to slither out as snakes, to jump out as frogs, to peep out and hide again as monkeys and to 'grow' out as plants moving towards the sun and opening their flowers.

Create stories with the children about what might have happened when particular storybook characters came out of their houses to go to work, to look for food or to visit their friends.

Extensions/Variations
Ask children to creep out while you shake a tambourine and to run back to their dens whenever you bang it suddenly.

Suggest that the children return to a different den each time, rather than their own

Learning objectives/Early Learning Goals
* Construct with a purpose in mind, using a variety of resources (EAD–EUMM)
* Use skills to explore concepts and ideas through representations (EAD–EUMM)
* Use available resources to create props to support role-play (EAD–BI)
* Work cooperatively, taking turns to use equipment and sharing resources (PSED–MR)
* Portray different characters through a variety of movements and actions (EAD–BI)
* Follow trails in character, exploring an outdoor or indoor area as an animal or a person from a story (UW–W; EAD–EUMM)
* Explore and develop skills of characterization within a small group, using different forms and language and intonation to imagine and recreate roles and experiences (CL–S)
* Notice changes in what is heard (CL–LA)

Make a scene

Themes
* Travelling/Places
* Seasons/Weather/Elements
* Times of Year/Celebrations

Skills
* Craftwork
* Group work
* Confidence
* Acting/Mime
* Movement/Dance

Equipment/Resources
A safe, clear space, on a wipe clean, hard floor surface, in which adults and children can spread out sheets and sit and move comfortably around them; old sheets and fabrics in white or plain colours and large pieces of plain card; markers and fabric pens and/or crayons; CD player; CDs featuring appropriate children's stories or songs; curtain or blanket, string and lamps

Activity
Discuss with the children a forthcoming performance or display that you are planning, to enhance the story or theme that you are exploring, and ask them to make their own drawings on sheets and card pieces, to be used as backcloths and set. Suggest that they make the designs bold and bright, without too many small details, so that they will be easily viewed by an audience and have a dramatic impact. Children may work individually, but encourage them to offer contributions to each other's designs. Make a rule that nobody may

draw over others' pictures and that drawings may only be changed or added to if all the artists agree. Places, such as forest, jungle, farm, beach or city, are easy for children to draw as large scenes but very effective, as are large vehicles, such as bus, train or ship. Seasons can be illustrated using appropriate colours and shapes and by including symbols such as kites flying in the wind and red, brown and orange leaves falling from trees.

Play a CD of the story or songs that you are illustrating and encourage children to join in and chant and sing together while they work.

Fasten the backcloths to the wall and perform dance sequences, musical numbers and shows in front of them. Add set pieces made from large pieces of card, designed by the children for their own use. Create a stage area by rigging a 'house tab' curtain on a string and using lamps. Invite families into the setting to watch performances.

Extensions/Variations
Provide the children with individual pieces of fabric and invite them to design their own pictures or patterns using only two colours, or one shape, or one number of their choice. Display these as a frieze or other arrangement along the wall, or use them as cloaks.

Keep the backcloths rolled up and ready for use in the role-play area and support children in fastening them to walls or draping them over furniture for their own performances.

Learning objectives/Early Learning Goals
* Explore and experiment to create different colours or textures (EAD–EUMM)
* Represent own ideas, thoughts and feelings through art and design (EAD–BI)
* Handle equipment and tools effectively, including pencils for drawing and writing (PD–MH)
* Work cooperatively, taking turns to use equipment and sharing resources (PSED–MR)
* Participate in a large group activity, understanding the need for rules and co-operation to ensure everybody's enjoyment (PSED–MR, MFB)
* Work, speak and listen appropriately as a member of a group, showing sensitivity to others' needs and feelings and responding with consideration (PSED–MR)
* Develop and act out an experience, a storyline or a narrative, working cooperatively within a group, and practise skills to perform before others with confidence (EAD–BI; PSED–SCSA)
* Memorize simple dances and confidently perform them to others, individually or within a group (EAD–EUMM; PSED–SCSA)

Bring on the rain

Themes
* Seasons/Weather/Elements
* Creatures/Animals/Birds/Plants

Skills
* Craftwork
* Listening
* Speech
* Singing

Equipment/Resources
Pots of water and clean paintbrushes; coloured pens or pencils; dry powder paints in various colours; coloured paper, white paper and silver foil or shiny paper; glue sticks and scissors; plastic spoons; music player; songs: We've Grown so Tall and Umbrella; instrumental track: Incy Wincy Spider (songs and instrumental track available to download from Brilliant Publications' website); CD player and CD collections of children's songs and popular music

Activity
Encourage children to make rainy day and puddle pictures by cutting irregular shapes from silver foil or shiny paper and gluing them onto coloured paper, then drawing people or animals splashing in them, or rain falling onto umbrellas and trees.

Show children how to make pictures of reflections often seen in puddles by painting sheets of white paper with clean water, then tipping very small spoonfuls of dry coloured powder paints onto the wet papers and shaking them gently to make them spread.

Read stories about rain and how it affects animals, birds and other creatures. Some, like ducks and frogs, enjoy it. Others, such as animals with fur and mini-beasts, take shelter until it stops. Encourage children to discuss the stories and to act some of them out.

Extensions/Variations
Challenge practitioners and children to think of as many rhymes and songs about rain as they can and sing or chant them together as a group. Some ideas might be: We've Grown so Tall; Umbrella; It's Raining, It's Pouring; I Hear Thunder; Rain, Rain, Go Away and Incy Wincy Spider.

There are also many popular songs, not specifically intended for children, that mention rain. These could be collected and recorded by a practitioner in advance and played as appropriate background music while children engage in their craft work

Learning objectives/Early Learning Goals
* Use simple tools and techniques competently and appropriately (EAD–EUMM)
* Capture experiences and responses with a range of media (EAD–BI)
* Create simple representations of events, people and objects (EAD–BI)
* Confidently try new activities, choose resources independently and say when do or don't need help (PSED–SCSA)
* Listen to stories, songs or rhymes with increasing attention and recall, in order to discuss and recreate all or parts of them (CL–LA)
* Speak clearly in unison (CL–S; PSED–SCSA)
* Join in with repeated refrains and anticipate key events and phrases in rhymes and songs (CL–LA)
* Add to a growing repertoire of familiar songs to be used in a variety of situations and activities (EAD–EUMM)

Firework night

Themes
* Times Of Year/Celebrations
* Colours/Shapes/Numbers
* Music/Sound

Skills
* Craftwork
* Movement/Dance

Equipment/Resources
A clear space in which adults and children can move around easily and safely; CD player; CDs featuring appropriate music, songs or sounds for a firework display or celebration; coloured ribbons (or pieces of fabric or chiffon scarves) attached to sticks; cardboard tubes, plastic straws and paper fasteners; black, coloured and shiny card and papers; white and coloured chalks, pencils and paints; scissors, glue sticks and sticky tape; shiny and coloured stickers – stars, spots and other shapes; pictures of fireworks

Activity
Discuss fireworks and look at pictures together. Provide large sheets of black card or paper and invite children to cover them in fireworks from their memories and imaginations, using chalks, pencils and sticky stars and shapes. Offer watery coloured paints and plastic straws and suggest that they drip colours onto the black paper and then blow them. Talk about the colours, shapes and patterns and children's previous experiences of fireworks.

Use cardboard tubes to make firework rockets. Cut circles of card, make them into cones and attach them to the tops of the tubes with sticky tape, tape a straw to the inside, leaving a length to form a stick, and then decorate the tubes. To make firework fountains, cut thin strips of coloured paper, curl them, tape them inside a cardboard tube and attach star stickers to the ends. Attach strips of shiny paper to straw sticks to make sparklers. Cut two circles, decorate them with stars and strips of paper that stick out around the edges. Insert a paper fastener through the middle and turn them separately to form a spinning Catherine wheel.

Play suitable music or sounds and dance with ribbons to create a firework display. Plan and discuss movements together. Move your fireworks around and make them 'whoosh' within the dance too, as long as the children understand never to touch a real firework and that they really move by themselves. Emphasize potential dangers and safety rules.

Extensions/Variations
Create a display with all of the children's pictures and fireworks and encourage them to write their names and other labels and captions to add to it. Encourage them to try to work out how they might spell words such as 'whoosh', 'pop', 'bang' and 'sparks'.

Invite families into the setting to watch the children's firework display performance, danced in front of their art display as a backcloth.

Learning objectives/Early Learning Goals
* Choose particular colours or materials to use for a purpose (EAD–BI)
* Use simple tools and techniques competently and appropriately (EAD–EUMM)
* Use and name shapes appropriately in creative tasks (M–SSM)
* Use identifiable letters and phonic knowledge to communicate meaning (L–W)
* Write own name and labels and captions (L–W)
* Interact as a member of a group to develop and act out a narrative through dance (EAD–BI)

There's a troll

Themes
* Stories/Fairy Tales
* Building/Homes
* Creatures/Animals/Birds/Plants

Skills
* Craftwork
* Acting/Mime
* Movement/Dance
* Group work

Equipment/Resources
A large enough room, with a safe space for a group of children to stand at each end; white and coloured paper and card; craft pieces, such as stickers, wool, foam shapes, buttons, cotton wool, felt and fabric scraps; craft matchsticks, straws and/or pipe cleaners; shirring or cord elastic; coloured pens, sticky tape and scissors; PVA glue and spreaders; plastic toy goats; a version of the story The Billy Goats Gruff; a microphone (real or toy)

Activity
Support the children in making scary troll masks to wear. Trim squares or rectangles of card to size, then invite them to draw face shapes, cut them out and decorate them, attaching pieces with glue and sticky tape, drawing and colouring. Refer to the pictures in the book for ideas if necessary, but encourage children to be original and not to copy the troll in the book. Practitioners can fasten elastic through the masks to fit the children's heads.

Invite the children to form two groups and stand at the ends of the room, wearing their troll masks. Encourage them to carefully and slowly creep backwards towards each other without turning around. When they sense that they are close enough (or gently bump into each other), they can turn around and scare each other by roaring, waving their arms, stamping their feet, jumping up and down, etc – anything except touching each other!

Ensure that all children are gentle and careful and that the 'scariness' is truly acting. Reassure or comfort any children who are worried or afraid and don't insist that any child joins in if they don't want to.

Extensions/Variations
Make bridges using craft matchsticks, straws or pipe cleaners, card and paper. Some children may build constructions using straws or pipe cleaners and sticky tape; others may cut rectangular lengths of paper or card and glue matchsticks or straws to them. Test the bridges to find out whether they are strong enough by standing plastic toy goats on them.

Re-enact the story with toys and props.

Provide a microphone and allow children to experiment with speaking in scary troll voices, if they wish to.

Learning objectives/Early Learning Goals
* Use available resources to create costume pieces and props to support role-play (EAD–BI)
* Portray characters and emotions through mime and expressive movement, understanding that the body can be used for communication (EAD–BI)
* Match movements and actions to the space available (PD–MH)
* Maintain attention, concentrate and move or stop quietly when appropriate (CL–LA)
* Select and use technology for particular purposes (UW–T)

Mask the effect

Themes
* Nursery Rhymes/Poems/Songs
* Creatures/Animals/Birds/Plants
* Stories/Fairy Tales
* People Who Help Us/Occupations

Skills
* Craftwork
* Singing
* Speech

Equipment/Resources
A clear space in which adults and children can work together comfortably as a group and move around safely and easily; white and coloured card and paper; paper plates; felt and fabric scraps; shirring or cord elastic; scissors, glue sticks and sticky tape; stickers, pipe cleaners, straws, feathers, ribbons, etc; coloured pens

Activity
Invite children to make masks for animals, birds, mini-beasts and other creatures, developing their own ideas, drawing details and cutting out ears, noses, whiskers, antennae, etc to attach to paper plates or card shapes. Practitioners should offer support, especially in cutting out the eyeholes and attaching elastic to fit each child's head and in labelling the masks with their names. If any children dislike wearing masks over their faces, suggest that they make a hat or a wig instead, or attach their mask to a stick made from pipe cleaners or straws and hold it up beside them as a friend.

Gather everybody together with their masks and discuss the different animals, birds and creatures represented. Challenge children to think of as many different rhymes and songs as they can involving the characters of the masks and then to perform them to the group. Many of these may be number rhymes, as so many creatures appear in them. For example: two little dicky birds, three little monkeys, five little speckled frogs, five or six little ducks. Songs can be fairly loosely connected if necessary, and you can always use a verse of Walking Through the Jungle to include any animal or creature.

End the activity with a whole group rendition of Old MacDonald Had a Farm, involving each animal, bird or other creature (or small group of them) in turn. Encourage the children to listen carefully and take cues, jumping up when they hear their character's name, to make appropriate noises or movements.

Extensions/Variations
Prepare identical masks for children (or dolls and teddies) to wear when acting out counting and number rhymes.

Make masks with hats depicting people pursuing different occupations, such as police officers, fire fighters, chefs or horse-riders, and act out poems and stories in character.

Learning objectives/Early Learning Goals
* Use available resources to create costume pieces and props to support role-play (EAD–BI)
* Choose particular colours or materials to use for a purpose (EAD–BI)
* Handle equipment and tools effectively, including pencils for drawing and writing (PD–MH)
* Use intonation and different voices in action and character songs (CL–S)
* Confidently use songs and rhymes that involve number names, counting on and counting back in ones, twos, fives and tens (M—N)
* Take cues to imitate, fill in or continue words or phrases in a song (CL–LA)
* Speak confidently within a familiar group and take turns to initiate discussion, describe an activity or perform a speech, song or rhyme, asking for help if needed (PSED–SCSA)

Puppet theatre

Themes
* Nursery Rhymes/Poems/Songs
* Stories/Fairy Tales

Skills
* Craftwork
* Confidence
* Speech
* Singing
* Acting/Mime

Equipment/Resources
A clear space in which adults and children can work together comfortably as a group; white and coloured card and paper; cardboard tubes, paper bags; felt and fabric pieces; old socks and gloves; scissors, glue, spreaders and sticky tape; stickers, pipe cleaners, straws, feathers, ribbons, wool, etc; coloured pens

Activity
Invite children to make puppets to act out rhymes, poems and songs. Offer a free choice of base materials, such as tubes, bags, fabric, card and socks, and craft resources to make features, limbs, hair, etc. Support children as they design and create their own characters. Practitioners could work alongside children, making other useful characters, such as a farmer, a baker, a baby and a wolf, or ordinary people who could play a variety of parts.

Bring together children with appropriate puppets, such as a cat and a queen or Humpty Dumpty, a horse and a soldier, and suggest that they act out a particular rhyme or song.

Suggest a popular story or fairy tale, such as Puss In Boots, to a group of children who have a cat puppet, a giant or ogre puppet, a king and a princess. Offer them some other people puppets who could play the parts of the miller and his sons and the field workers and support them in remembering and re-enacting the story.

Extensions/Variations
Ask children to make up their own poems, songs and stories for their puppets. Encourage them to move around and work in different groups to explore the characters they have made.

Play circle games in which each person has a puppet and speaks or sings as that character instead of himself. This is a safe way for children to try out the feelings involved in being a little bit naughty or cheeky, not very clever, especially chatty or very bossy and can be great fun, although adults should always discourage speech or behaviour that is rude or too silly. Shy and under-confident children often find their voices through puppets and begin to participate at levels that they are not yet able to achieve as themselves.

Learning objectives/Early Learning Goals
* Use media and materials in original ways to suit different uses or purposes (EAD–BI)
* Work cooperatively, taking turns to use equipment and sharing resources (PSED–MR)
* Improve confidence and social skills through participation in a large group activity (PSED–MR, MFB; PD–MH)
* Use language to imagine and recreate ideas and experiences for acting and role-play (CL–S)
* Explore and develop skills of characterization within a small group, by representing own ideas, thoughts and feelings through music, dance and role play while acting out a familiar storyline within a song (EAD–BI)
* Develop and act out a storyline or a narrative, working cooperatively within a group, and practise skills to perform before others with confidence (EAD–BI; PSED–SCSA)

Topic index

All of the activities within the book can be made relevant to two or more different themes, so, whatever the topic you are studying, or the children would like to study, you can find a variety of suggestions within this book. Activities are listed in alphabetical order.

Topic index

Drama Activities for the Early Years
© Debbie Chalmers and Brilliant Publications

Times of Year/Celebrations

Travelling/Places

Suggested stories, songs, rhymes and music for use with the activities

Suggested well-known stories for use within activities

Bears in the Night by Stan and Jan Berenstain (Harper Collins) - page 83

Bertha stories (various) by Eric Charles and Steve Augard (Hippo Books) – page 37

Bob The Builder stories (various) by Diane Redmond (BBC Worldwide) – page 80

Dr Seuss stories (various) (Random House Inc.) – page 37

The Very Hungry Caterpillar by Eric Carle (Puffin) – page 27

We're Going On A Bear Hunt by Michael Rosen and Helen Oxenbury (Walker Books) - page 83

Where The Wild Things Are by Maurice Sendak (Harper Collins) – page 83

Songs available to download as e-resources from Brilliant Publications' website (for a small fee)

Aeroplane – pages 40, 60

Click Your Fingers – pages 30, 48, 54, 78

'Hello' – Bounce – page 56

I've Got One Head – pages 48, 54, 91

Shake 'n' Rattle – pages 26, 53, 66

Shaker Song – pages 25, 48, 54

The Train – pages 32, 40, 53, 60

Toes and Knees – pages 48, 91

Umbrella – pages 33, 44, 96

We've Grown so Tall – pages 25, 33, 75, 96

Windows – pages 40, 41, 53, 60

Your Shoes – pages 30, 53

Note: These songs originally appeared in **Start with a Song** by Mavis de Mierre, published by Brilliant Publications).

Well-known and traditional songs mentioned by name:

*Indicates that an instrumental version is available to download as an e-resource from the Brilliant Publications' website (for a small fee)

Baa Baa Black Sheep – page 52, 64

Barney the Dinosaur (various songs) – page 91

Bertha the Big Machine (various songs) – page 37

Bob the Builder (various songs) – page 80

Build it Up – page 80

Clap Your Hands – page 38

Farmer's in his Den – page 88

Five Currant Buns – page 50

Five Little Ducks Went Swimming One Day – page 33

Five Little Speckled Frogs – pages 33, 50*

Head, Shoulders, Knees and Toes – page 48*

Here We Go Round the Mulberry Bush – pages 53, 88

Hey Diddle Diddle – page 38

Hot Cross Buns – page 58, 64

How Do You Feel Today? – page 38

Humpty Dumpty – page 55, 64, 68

I Hear Thunder – page 96

If You're Happy and You Know it – pages 38, 46*

I'm a Little Teapot – page 73

I'm Going to Build a Little House – page 80

In and Out the Dusty Bluebells – page 88

Incy Wincy Spider – pages 52, 64, 68, 96*

It's Raining, It's Pouring – page 96

Jack and Jill – pages 32, 55

Jelly on a Plate – page 64

Little Miss Muffet – page 38

Let's Go Walking – page 53

London Bridge – page 80*

Old MacDonald Had a Farm – page 99

One Brick at a Time from Barnum – page 28

One Potato, Two Potato – page 58

Oranges and Lemons – page 88

Peter Works with One Hammer – page 68

Polly Put the Kettle On – page 58*

Rain, Rain, Go Away – page 96

Ring a Ring a Roses – pages 49, 88

Row, Row, Row Your Boat – pages 31, 72

Round and Round the Village – page 88

She'll Be Coming Round the Mountain – pages 32, 53

Sweet Gingerbread Man – page 58

Note

To download songs and instrumental tracks from Brilliant Publications' website, you will need Acrobat Reader 9, which can be downloaded for free from the Internet.

Brilliant Publications' website:
www.brilliantpublications.co.uk